Old Testament Survey

Part I

Genesis:
The Family Of God

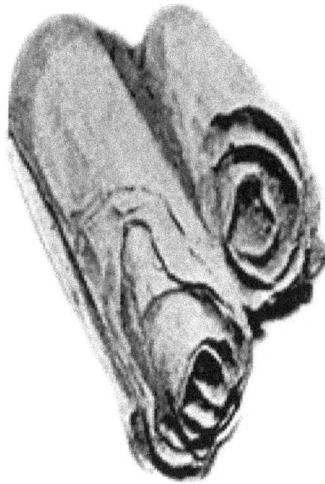

Dr. C.V. White

Old Testament Survey Part I: Genesis: The Family of God
Dr. Cynthia V. White

Unless otherwise quoted all word definitions Greek and Hebrew and scripture quotations are from the King James Version of the Bible as recorded in the Blue Letter Bible: Retrieved from http://www.blueletterbible.org. All other scripture quotations from the amplified Bible were retrieved from the biblegateway.com by the Lockman Foundation or International Standard Bible Encyclopedia, Electronic Database, Copyright © 1995-1996, 2003 by Biblesoft, Inc., All rights reserved, The New Unger's Bible Dictionary - Originally published by Moody Press of Chicago, Illinois, Copyright © 1988.Research definitions from Wikipedia, the free encyclopedia, Nelson's Illustrated Bible Dictionary.

Published by:

Fruit That Remain, LLC
150 Post Office Road Suite 1027
Waldorf, Maryland
http://cvwhite.com
Email: drcvwhite@gmail.com

ISBN-13: 978-1-934326-07-7
ISBN-10: 1-934326-07-0
Copyright @ 2016 by Fruit That Remain Publishing

DiViNE Purpose Publishing Co., LLC
www.divinepurposepublishing.com
info@divinepurposepublishing.com

Printed in the United States of America

DEDICATION

This book is dedicated my biological father, Rev. Lee Andrew Townes Sr., who helped me to mature naturally and spiritually. He is the seed from which I came. My father was an inspiration to me as my father and as my pastor for many years. He started to preach when he was eight years old and continued for seventy-two years. For fifty of those years he pastored churches, and during that time he was instrumental in the spiritual growth of many aspiring pastors and clergy. Also, I thank Bishop Rodney S. Walker, I, my spiritual father, who has been instrumental in my spiritual growth. Bishop Walker, I appreciate your support while I was attending school, working, and preparing for ministry. You have been and still are a great blessing to me! Every step of the way you encouraged me to continue with my writing projects. I am appreciative of all of your efforts to assist me in this project and in other areas of my life. I also appreciate God for giving me such a wonderful spiritual father in you! You are a special gift from God and I will always cherish everything that you have poured into me all of these years.

I want to thank my Mother Cynthia Ollie Mary Townes Turner for giving birth to me and helping me in every way she possible could. I want to thank my niece Cynthia Anglin, my Children, Myrna White, Gregory T. White Jr. and Lance White, Larry White, Laura White and Denise, and all of their children and the generations that follow to let them know how much I appreciate them and God for making it possible for all of them to be a part of me.

A special thank you to my niece Cynthia Anglin for her support and her prayers for me and my projects, I appreciate her help and support.

APPRECIATION

I would like to take this opportunity to thank Fruit That Remain Publishing LLC, Bishop Rodney S. Walker, I., Paulette Walker, Lisa Burgess, the Old Testament Survey Class of 2014 and 2015 for their support and assistance in the preparation of this book for publication.

I appreciate your willingness to meet the challenges necessary to complete the final preparation for printing and distribution. Your ideas and suggestions contributed immensely to the success of this project. It was so good to have you as part of the team. I am confident that good things will come from our joint efforts. Thank you, again, for a job well done!

TABLE OF CONTENTS

Old Testament Survey

Part I

Genesis:
The Family Of God

CHAPTER 1

THE DATELESS PAST
(THE TIME BEFORE HISTORY)

The Time Before Adam (Chapter 1:1-2)

Genesis is considered by theologians and historians as a book of beginnings. According to popular beliefs it is the beginning of the earth and its inhabitants, the first man being Adam. However, we know that there is evidence of the existence of prehistoric people and animals, better known to some of us as cave men and dinosaurs. As believers we should have an answer for the existence of things that happened before history. When we try to say that Adam was the first man on earth the historians will get the best of us because they have the fossils of what they called cave men and other animals including dinosaurs.

Prehistoric means before history and history started with Adam. God did not leave us ignorant of what happened before history. We just had to dig deep into His Word to find the answer.

When I was in elementary school we were confronted with this question because we were being taught Darwin's theory - **Darwinism is a theory of biological evolution developed by Charles Darwin and others, stating that all species of organisms arise and develop through the natural selection of small, inherited variations that increase the individual's ability to compete, survive, and reproduce, also called Darwinian Theory. It originally included the broad concepts of transmutation of species or of evolution which gained general scientific acceptance when Charles Robert Darwin published On the Origin of Species.**

This was the true understanding of how the world explained our existence, but we as believers were taught that God created everything including man and there was no such thing as natural selection or evolution. God did it and that was what happened, but we could not explain the prehistoric factor. I decided that maybe they came up with that theory because God said that one day was as a thousand years and in Genesis chapter 1 God was working on one day at a time and as a child that made sense to me. I still thought that God had done it and since He was talking about what happened on the 1st day and the 2nd day and so on that each one of those days must have been 1000 years. My explanation was not correct but at least I knew that Darwin was wrong.

What happened between Genesis chapter 1 verse 1 and verse 2 is all about the beginning of things and what happened to the prehistoric times. There was an enormous amount of time between these 2 verses and the events that took place before verse 3. We will find when we examine this information that Noah's flood was not the first flood.

I remember when my husband and I took our children on vacation to the Dinosaur National Monument located in the states of Utah and Colorado. There are over 1,500 dinosaur fossils visible in the cliff face. We were able to see them and the park rangers reported to us that they were all drowned under water and got lodged in mud that eventually became exposed in what is now rock after 149 million years. We were able to touch the huge bones that they said were 149 million years old. I wondered how so many land animals got under water and stuck in the mud at the bottom of whatever water that was. But now I know that it was a flood orchestrated by God and that it was a flood before history was recorded.

Let me explain to you the assignment of the God Head - **Jehovah** – God our Father's assignment is to create and destroy, in the Old Testament that is all you will see Him doing, the assignment of **the Son (Christ)** is to Save and Redeem. He is seen in the Old Testament in types, shadows and like as. One example of that in the Old Testament is Moses being a type of Christ, but the New Testament is all about Him. The assignment of **Holy Spirit** is to maintain what was redeemed and saved. He is our Comforter, Paraclete, Advocate and Helper and He is still doing all of that today.

Jehovah – Creator and Destroyer – God is leading all of His creation to His expected end (God is Making His creations His sons). His original intent is that His creation stays in fellowship with Him. However, it must be of their free will and if evil is the choice of their free will, and He protects His holy seed until the time of redemption and salvation.

[Jhn 1:1-3 KJV] [1] In the beginning was the Word, and the Word was with God, and the Word was God. [2] The same was in the beginning with God. [3] All things were made by him; and without him was not any thing made that was made.

- **Flood of Noah** – Was not the first flood, but it is the last for the purpose it was used by God. **[Gen 5:29, 32 KJV] [29]** And he called his name Noah, saying, This [same] shall comfort us concerning our work and toil of our hands, because of the ground which the LORD hath cursed. ... ³² And Noah was five hundred years old: and Noah begat Shem, Ham, and Japheth. **[Gen 6:17 KJV]** ¹⁷ And, behold, I, even I, do bring a flood of waters upon the earth, to destroy all flesh, wherein [is] the breath of life, from under heaven; [and] everything that [is] in the earth shall die. **[Gen 9:11 KJV]** ¹¹ And I will establish my covenant with you; neither shall all flesh be cut off any more by the waters of a flood; neither shall there anymore be a flood to destroy the earth.

Jehovah started over with Noah. He destroyed what was not like He needed it to be and started over with Noah. Now He wants to start over with Moses.

- *[Deu 9:8, 14 KJV]* ⁸ Also in Horeb ye provoked the LORD to wrath, so that the LORD was angry with you to have destroyed you. ... ¹⁴ Let me alone, that I may destroy them, and blot out their name from under heaven: and I will make of thee a nation mightier and greater than they. In this passage Jehovah wanted to destroy them and start over with Moses but Moses interceded for them as a type of Christ and the LORD repented, in other words decided not to do it. Remember His assignment is to create and destroy.

Dateless Past Before the Recreation

As you read the following passages you will notice none of these things has happened since Adam. All of this had to happen before Adam. These passages were written by different people at different times. The LORD gives them all the same information. When did the entire earth shake back and forth since Adam? When were the water channels seen and foundations of the world discovered since Adam? When was the earth empty since Adam? When was the earth turned upside down since Adam? The earth is two thirds water and if it is turned upside down that had to cause a huge flood all of this was before Adam. When did the LORD take hold of the ends of the earth and shook the wicked out of it since Adam?

As believers we get all kinds of explanations for things that we have not researched the bible to get the answers. One of them is the origin of the stars and the heaven that we can see and the constellations. We should be able to go into the bible and find out what God said about them instead we rely on things like scientific explanations or Greek mythology. Take a look at the passages below and see where the LORD mentions them and understand that He made it all. No one else can get the credit although many will try. Even things like the ice age can be explained in the bible but no one will ever use the bible to explain these things if believers don't. You can tell them when all of the water was frozen and the earth was a frozen wasteland because that is found in Job. The LORD asked Job "Out of whose womb came the ice? and the hoary frost of heaven, who hath gendered it? The waters are hid as [with] a stone, and the face of the deep is frozen." There is much more in the bible to help us understand what the LORD did in Genesis but we have to search for it and believe that it is there. As you read these passages look for things that have not happened since Adam and also notice that the same words of what happened before Adam were given to different people at different times. The LORD wanted to make sure that we as His people knew what happened.

Take a look at these passages:

- **[Psa 18:7-15 KJV]** 7 Then **the earth (the Hebrew for earth is ''erets' = ground, surface of the earth) shook (the Hebrew for shook is 'ga`ash' = (Hithpael) to shake back and forth, toss or reel to and fro) and trembled (the Hebrew of trembled is 'ra`ash' = (Niphal) to be made to quake); the foundations also of the hills (the Hebrew for hills is 'har' = hill, mountain, hill country, mount) moved (the Hebrew for moved is 'ragaz' = tremble, quake, rage, quiver, be agitated, be excited, be perturbed) and were shaken, because he was wroth.** 8 There went up a smoke out of his nostrils, and fire out of his mouth devoured: coals were kindled by it. 9 He **bowed** (the Hebrew for bowed is **natah = to stretch out, extend, stretch, offer)** the **heavens** (the Hebrew for heavens is **shamayim = as abode of the stars as the visible universe, the sky, atmosphere, etc)** also, **and came down: and darkness [was] under his feet.** 10 And he rode upon a cherub, and did fly: yea, he did fly upon the wings of the wind. 11 He made darkness his secret place; **his pavilion round about him [were] dark waters [and] thick clouds of the skies. 12 At the brightness [that was] before him his thick clouds passed, hail [stones] and coals of fire. 13 The LORD also thundered in the heavens, and** the Highest gave his voice; hail [stones] and coals of fire. 14 Yea, he sent out his arrows, and scattered them; and he shot out lightnings, and discomfited them. 15 **Then the channels of waters were seen, and the foundations of the world were discovered at thy rebuke,** O LORD, at the blast of the breath of thy nostrils.

- **[2Sa 22:8, 16 KJV]** 8 Then the earth shook and trembled; the foundations of heaven moved and shook, because he was wroth. ... 16 And the channels of the sea appeared, the foundations of the world were discovered, at the rebuking of the LORD, at the blast of the breath of his nostrils.

- **[Psa 18:7, 15 KJV]** 7 Then the earth shook and trembled; the foundations also of the hills moved and were shaken, because he was wroth. ... 15 Then the channels of waters were seen, and the foundations of the world were discovered at thy rebuke, O LORD, at the blast of the breath of thy nostrils.

- **[2Sa 22:8-16 KJV]** 8 Then the earth shook and trembled; the foundations of heaven moved and shook, because he was wroth. 9 There went up a smoke out of his nostrils, and fire out of his mouth devoured: coals were kindled by it. 10 He bowed the heavens also, and came down; and darkness [was] under his feet. 11 And he rode upon a cherub, and did fly: and he was seen upon the wings of the wind. 12 And he made darkness pavilions round about him, dark waters, [and] thick clouds of the skies. 13 Through the brightness before him were coals of fire kindled. 14 The LORD thundered from heaven, and the most High uttered his voice. 15 And he sent out arrows, and scattered them; lightning, and discomfited them. 16 And the channels of the sea appeared, the foundations of the world were discovered, at the rebuking of the LORD, at the blast of the breath of his nostrils.

- **[Isa 24:1-7 KJV]** 1 Behold, the LORD maketh the earth empty, and maketh it waste, and turneth it upside down, and scattereth abroad the inhabitants thereof.(The LORD has not made the earth empty or made it a waste or turned it upside down since Adam, This has not been done since Adam, this was before Adam) 2 And it shall be, as with the people, so with the priest; as with the servant, so with his master; as with the maid, so with her mistress; as with the buyer, so with the seller; as with the lender, so with the borrower; as with the taker of usury, so with the giver of usury to him. 3 The land shall be utterly emptied, and utterly spoiled: for the LORD hath spoken this word. 4 The earth mourneth [and] fadeth away, the world languisheth [and] fadeth away, the haughty people of the earth do languish. 5 The earth also is defiled under the inhabitants thereof; because they have transgressed the laws, changed the ordinance, broken the everlasting covenant. 6 Therefore hath the curse devoured the earth, and they that dwell therein are desolate: therefore the inhabitants of the earth are burned, and few men left. 7 The new wine mourneth, the vine languisheth, all the merryhearted do sigh.

- **[Job 38:1-41 KJV]** 1 Then the LORD answered Job out of the whirlwind, and said, 2 Who [is] this that darkeneth counsel by words without knowledge? 3 Gird up now thy loins like a man; for I will demand of thee, and answer thou me. 4 Where wast thou when I laid the foundations of the earth? declare, if thou hast understanding. 5 Who hath laid the measures thereof, if thou knowest? or who hath stretched the line upon it? 6 Whereupon are the foundations thereof fastened? or who laid the corner stone thereof; 7 When the morning stars sang together, and all the sons of God shouted for joy? 8 Or [who] shut up the sea with doors, when it brake forth, [as if] it had issued out of the womb? 9 When I made the cloud the garment thereof, and thick darkness a swaddling band for it, 10 And brake up for it my decreed [place], and set bars and doors, 11 And said, Hitherto shalt thou come, but no further: and here shall thy proud waves be stayed? 12 Hast thou commanded the morning since thy days; [and] caused the dayspring to know his place; 13 That it might take hold of the ends of the earth, that the wicked might be shaken out of it? 14 It is turned as clay [to] the seal; and they stand as a garment. 15 And from the wicked their light is withholden, and the high arm shall be broken. 16 Hast thou entered into the springs of the sea? or hast thou walked in the search of the depth? 17 Have the gates of death been opened unto thee? or hast thou seen the doors of the shadow of death? 18 Hast thou perceived the breadth of the earth? declare if thou knowest it all. 19 Where [is] the way [where] light dwelleth? and [as for] darkness, where [is] the place thereof, 20 That thou shouldest take it to the bound thereof, and that thou shouldest know the paths [to] the house thereof? 21 Knowest thou [it], because thou wast then born? or [because] the number of thy days [is] great? 22 Hast thou entered into the treasures of the snow? or hast thou seen the treasures of the hail, 23 Which I have reserved against the time of trouble, against the day of battle and war? 24 By what way is the light parted, [which] scattereth the east wind upon the earth? 25 Who hath divided a watercourse for the overflowing of waters, or a way for the lightning of thunder; 26 To cause it to rain on the earth, [where] no man [is; on] the wilderness, wherein [there is] no man; 27 To satisfy the desolate and waste [ground]; and to cause the bud of the tender herb to spring forth? 28 Hath the rain a father? or who hath begotten the drops of dew? 29 Out of whose womb came the ice? and the hoary frost of heaven, who hath gendered it? 30 The waters are hid as [with] a stone, and the face of the deep is frozen. 31 Canst thou bind the sweet influences of Pleiades, or loose the bands of Orion? 32 Canst thou bring forth Mazzaroth in his season? or canst thou guide Arcturus with his sons? 33 Knowest thou the ordinances of heaven? canst thou set the dominion thereof in the earth? 34 Canst thou lift up thy voice to the clouds, that abundance of waters may cover thee? 35 Canst thou send lightnings, that they may go, and say unto thee, Here we [are]? 36 Who hath put wisdom in the inward parts? or who hath given understanding to the heart? 37 Who can number the clouds in wisdom? or who can stay the bottles of heaven, [38] When the dust groweth into hardness, and the clods cleave fast together? [39] Wilt thou hunt the prey for the lion? or fill the appetite of the young lions, [40] When they couch in [their] dens, [and] abide in the covert to lie in wait? [41] Who provideth for the raven his food? when his young ones cry unto God, they wander for lack of meat.

This information on the constellations and the ice age was taken from Wikipedia, the free encyclopedia:

Orion is a prominent constellation located on the celestial equator and visible throughout the world. It is one of the most conspicuous and recognizable constellations in the night sky. God called this constellation Orion but Wikipedia reports it as being named after Orion, a hunter in Greek mythology. Its brightest stars are Rigel (Beta Orionis) and Betelgeuse (Alpha Orionis), a blue-white and a red supergiant.

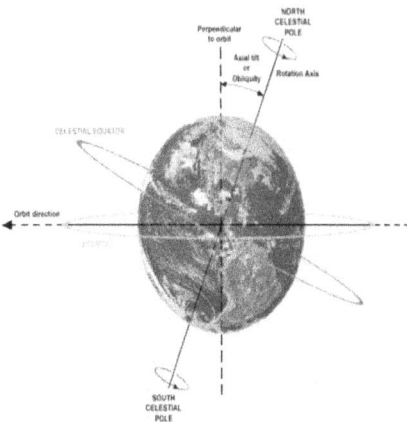

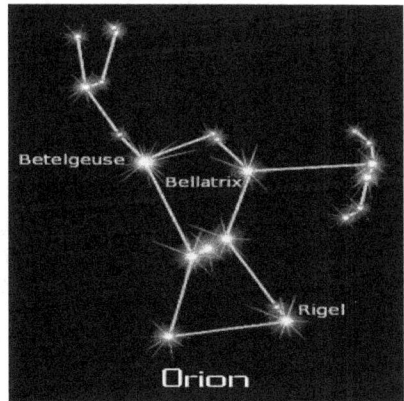

Job 9:9 Which maketh Arcturus, Orion, and Pleiades, and the chambers of the south. KJV

Job 38:31 Canst thou bind the sweet influences of Pleiades, or loose the bands of Orion? KJV

Amos 5:8 Seek him that maketh the seven stars and Orion, and turneth the shadow of death into the morning, and maketh the day dark with night: that calleth for the waters of the sea, and poureth them out upon the face of the earth: The LORD is his name: KJV

There are 88 officially recognized constellations, covering the entire sky. When astronomers say an object is "in" a given constellation, they mean it is within the boundaries of one of these defined areas of sky.

The Pleiades (/'plaɪ.ədiːz/ or /'pliː.ədiːz/), or Seven Sisters, is an open star cluster containing middle-aged hot B-type stars located in the constellation of Taurus. It is among the nearest star clusters to Earth and is the cluster most obvious to the naked eye in the night sky.

Arcturus is a red giant star in the Northern Hemisphere of Earth's sky that is the brightest star in the constellation Boötes

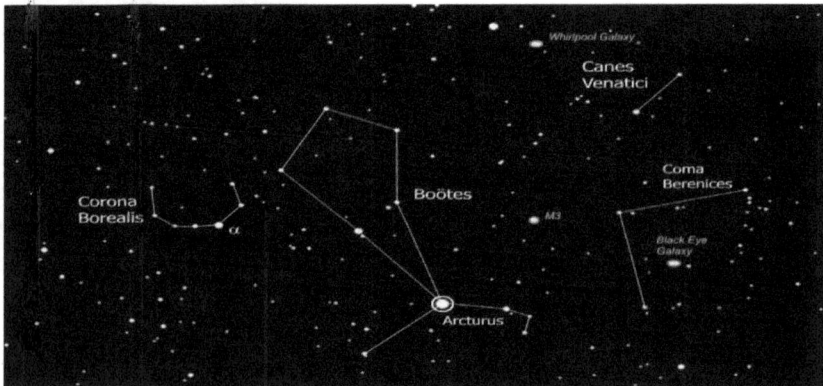

What about the ice age? An ice age is a period of long-term reduction in the temperature of Earth's surface and atmosphere, resulting in the presence or expansion of continental and polar ice sheets and alpine glaciers. Within a long-term ice age, individual pulses of cold climate are termed "glacial periods" (or alternatively "glacials" or "glaciations" or colloquially as "ice age"), and intermittent warm periods are called "interglacials". From a glaciological perspective the ice age implies the presence of extensive ice sheets in the northern and southern hemispheres. [1] By this definition, we are in an interglacial period—the holocene—of the ice age that began 2.6 million years ago at the start of the Pleistocene epoch, because the Greenland, Arctic, and Antarctic ice sheets still exist.[2]

[Isa 13:7-15 KJV] **7** Therefore shall all hands be faint, and every man's heart shall melt: **8** And they shall be afraid: pangs and sorrows shall take hold of them; they shall be in pain as a woman that travaileth: they shall be amazed one at another; their faces [shall be as] flames. **9 Behold, the day of the LORD cometh, cruel both with wrath and fierce anger, to lay the land (the Hebrew for land is ''erets' = whole earth (as opposed to a part) desolate (the Hebrew for desolate is 'shammah" = waste, horror, appalment): and he shall destroy (shamad = to destroy, exterminate, be destroyed, be exterminated) the sinners (thereof out of it. 10 For the stars of heaven and the constellations thereof shall not give their light: the sun shall be darkened in his going forth, and the moon shall not cause her light to shine.** The LORD in this passage is telling the stars, the constellations, the sun and the moon not to shine this has not happened since Adam, the heaven above the earth is now dark **11 And I will punish the world for [their] evil, and the wicked for their iniquity; and I will cause the arrogancy of the proud to cease, and will lay low the haughtiness of the terrible.** and move it **12** I will make a man more precious than fine gold; even a man than the golden wedge of Ophir. **13 Therefore I will shake the heavens, and the earth shall remove out of her place,** in the wrath of the LORD of hosts, and in the day of his fierce anger. *We see from this passage that the LORD is angry and He is about to flood the earth. The LORD goes on to say that He will make a man after this that will be very precious but for now He is about to shake the heavens and the earth shall move out of it place and that has not happened since Adam.* If the cavemen were those precious people they would still be here. The earth has not move out of its place since Adam **14** And it shall be as the chased roe, and as a sheep that no man taketh up: they shall every man turn to his own people, and flee every one into his own land. **15** Every one that is found shall be thrust through; and every one that is joined [unto them] shall fall by the sword. This is what it is going to feel like to the inhabitants.

The LORD was angry because of what Lucifer has done and that is the reason for this flood, notice what is said in this passage. Lucifer was in charge of the earth at this time and he did evil and caused the inhabitants to also do evil in the earth. The LORD wanted the earth to look like heaven. [Isa 14:12-21 KJV] **12 How art thou fallen from heaven, O Lucifer, son of the morning! [how] art thou cut down to the ground, which didst weaken the nations(Prophets)!** How was he able to weaken the nations? Lucifer is indicating that he is a prophet to the nations and in that position he can weaken them. Lucifer was on earth because that is where the people were. **13 For thou hast said in thine heart, I will ascend into heaven, I will exalt my throne** (this means that he had a throne and it was in the earth) above the stars of God: I will sit also upon **the mount of the congregation (Priest),** in the sides of the north: What congregation? The LORD has not given him that position since Adam **14 I will** ascend above the heights of the clouds; I will be like the most High. **15 Yet thou shalt be brought down to hell** (he is now dethroned and the LORD is flooding the earth and is going to start over with Adam, that precious man that He said He would make, just as He started over with Noah and was going to start over with Moses), **to the sides of the pit. 16 They that see thee shall** narrowly look upon thee, [and] consider thee, [saying, Is] this the man that made the earth to tremble, **that did shake kingdoms** (*and since he had a throne he was also a king with a kingdom*); **17** [That] **made the world as a wilderness, and destroyed the cities thereof; [that] opened not the house of his prisoners? 18 All the kings of the nations, [even] all of them, lie in glory, every one in his own house.** (Can you see all that happened here? The world as a wilderness and the cities destroyed. Lucifer is given credit for all of this) **19 But thou art cast out of thy grave like an abominable branch, [and as] the raiment of those that are slain, thrust through with a sword, that go down to the stones of the pit; as a carcase trodden under feet. 20 Thou shalt not be joined with them in burial, because thou hast destroyed thy land, [and] slain thy people: the seed of evildoers shall never be renowned. 21 Prepare slaughter for his children for the iniquity of their fathers; that they do not rise, nor possess the land, nor fill the face of the world with cities.**

In this passage the LORD showed Jeremiah what happened before Adam **[Jer 4:20-29 KJV] 20** Destruction upon destruction is cried; for the whole land is spoiled: suddenly are my tents spoiled, [and] my curtains in a moment. **21** How long shall I see the standard, [and] hear the sound of the trumpet? **22** For my people [is] foolish, they have not known me; they [are] sottish children, and they have none understanding: they [are] wise to do evil, but to do good they have no knowledge. **23 I beheld the earth, and, lo, [it was] without form, and void; and the heavens, and they [had] no light**. When since Adam was the earth without form and void and there was no light in the heavens? **24 I beheld the mountains, and, lo, they trembled, and all the hills moved lightly. 25 I beheld, and, lo, [there was] no man, and all the birds of the heavens were fled.** When since Adam was there no man on earth and no birds? **26 I beheld, and, lo, the fruitful place [was] a wilderness, and all the cities thereof were broken down at the presence of the LORD, [and] by his fierce anger.** Jeremiah saw the earth a fruitful place and he looked again and it was a wilderness and all the cities broken down, that has not happened since Adam, it had to be before Adam **27 For thus hath the LORD said, The whole land shall be desolate; yet will I not make a full end. 28 For this shall the earth mourn, and the heavens above be black: because I have spoken [it], I have purposed [it], and will not repent, neither will I turn back from it.** We can see from this passage that said that He did it all, He (Jehovah, the creator and destroyer) shut out the lights and made the heavens above the earth black and He goes on to say in the next verse that not a man shall dwell in the cities. That has not happen for

18

all of the cities since Adam. Then the LORD goes on to say that He will not fully destroy the earth, He leaves it in a condition where He can start over with Adam. **²⁹ The whole city shall flee for the noise of the horsemen and bowmen; they shall go into thickets, and climb up upon the rocks: every city [shall be] forsaken, and not a man dwell therein.**

Everything that God Himself did in the Old Testament is connected in some way to His order or His principles and we will point some of those out so that you will be able to recognized them as we continue through this survey. Christ can be found in each of the books of the Old Testament, and from time to time we will point that out so that you will know how to recognize Him and be able to find Him in the books that we do not cover if you desire to do so.

As we continue with our study we have to understand that the LORD has told the stars, constellations, sun and moon not to shine. He has literally cut off light; He had covered the earth, the literal ground which is the land with water. Now in Genesis chapter 1 He is going to give the light permission to shine and the ground permission to appear from under the water and prepare the earth to be inhabited which was always his intent as He said to Isaiah in - **Isa 45:18 KJV** For thus saith the LORD that created the heavens; God himself that formed the earth and made it; he hath established it, he created it not in vain, he formed it to be inhabited: I [am] the LORD; and [there is] none else.

EARTH – PLANTS – TREES – ANIMALS – FISH

❖ **Recreation** – Let is a word of permission. God gave everything permission to be and to do what He told it to do. There are 10 Let's between Gen 2:3-26:

1. And God said, Let there be light: and there was light. **[Gen 1:3 KJV]** – notice that God turned on the light but he does not mention the stars, constellations, sun or moon yet.

God in this verse is Elohim in the Hebrew it is the plurality of God the Father (Jehovah), the Son (Christ) and Holy Spirit, the God head. Notice (**And God said**) this is extremely important because this tie in with the understanding that God Exhausts His word above His name and why we must **say, speak, and declare**. Please note that Christ is not mentioned specifically because He is a part of the God Head Elohiym, but we know that the word of God is Christ.

> *In the beginning was the Word, and the Word was with God, and the Word was God. [Jhn 1:1 KJV]*

> *The same was in the beginning with God. [Jhn 1:2 KJV]*

> *All things were made by him; and without him was not any thing made that was made. [Jhn 1:3 KJV]*

2. And God said, **Let there be a firmament in the midst of the waters,** and let it divide the waters from the waters. **[Gen 1:6 KJV]**- The waters were one and were divided by a firmament

    [Northern Hemisphere at the top from midway up --- Southern Hemisphere from midway down, remember that ice we talked about where is it? The remainder of the ice at the top and that is called the North Pole and the ice at the bottom is called the South Pole.]

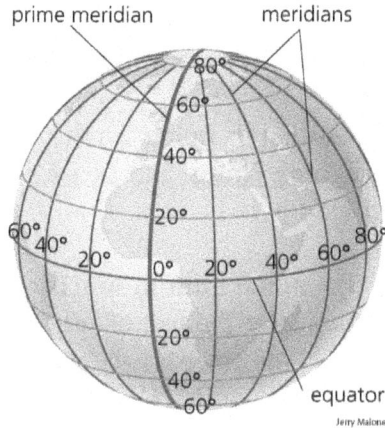

Earth Graphic by Jerry Malone

3. And God said, **Let the waters under the heaven be gathered together unto one place, and let the dry [land] appear:** and it was so. **[Gen 1:9 KJV]**

There was not dry land it was all water. The land had to appear, we know that Noah's flood is the only one that happened after Adam therefore, there must have been a flood because the earth was inhabited before Adam and now there is no dry land.

4. And God said, **Let the earth bring forth grass,** the herb yielding seed, [and] the fruit tree yielding fruit after his kind, whose seed [is] in itself, upon the earth: and it was so. **[Gen 1:11 KJV]** Notice the earth is bringing forth, God commanded the earth to bring forth. God has put something in the earth that gives it the ability to bring forth.

5. And God said, **Let there be lights in the firmament of the heaven to divide the day from the night;** and let them be for signs, and for seasons, and for days, and years: **[Gen 1:14 KJV]**.

Now that God has established the firmament He turned on the lights in for signs of seasons, days and years.

6. And let them be for **lights in the firmament of the heaven to give light upon the earth:** and it was so. **[Gen 1:15 KJV]** Now the light in the firmament gives light upon the earth.

7. And God said, **Let the waters bring forth abundantly** the moving creature that hath life, and fowl [that] may fly above the earth in the open firmament of heaven. **[Gen 1:20 KJV]** While the earth brings forth (grows things one at a time) the waters are commanded to bring forth large numbers swarms at a time.

8. And God blessed them, saying, Be fruitful, and multiply, and fill the waters in the seas, and **let fowl multiply in the earth**. **[Gen 1:22 KJV]**

9. And God said, **Let the earth bring forth** the <u>living creature</u> after his kind, **cattle**, and **creeping thing**, and **beast of the earth** after his kind: and it was so. **[Gen 1:24 KJV]**

10. And God said, **Let <u>US</u> make man in our image**, after our likeness: and let them have dominion over the fish of the sea, and over the fowl of the air, and over the cattle, and over all the earth, and over every creeping thing that creepeth upon the earth. **[Gen 1:26 KJV]**

The Hebrew word for make in this verse is `asah which means to do, fashion, accomplish, make. Notice what happened in Genesis chapter 2 verse 7 *And the LORD God formed man [of] the dust of the ground, and breathed into his nostrils the breath of life; and man became a living soul. [Gen 2:7 KJV]* Also notice that God did not say let the earth bring man forth, He said let us make man in our image and our likeness but He used the earth (soil, dust) to form him.

The soil is the lose dust the top layer of the earth, therefore we understand that God used the same lose soil to form man; in addition Gen. 2:7 also says that God formed man of the dust of the ground. The definition of ground in this verse comes from the Hebrew word **'adamah**, which is a feminine noun which means ground, land ground (as general, tilled, yielding sustenance) piece of ground, a specific plot of land, earth substance (for building or constructing), ground as earth's visible surface, land, territory, country, whole inhabited earth. This **adamah** is the substance that grows things. God formed man of the dust of the **adamah** and God called him Adam. We know that God had deposited substances in the earth that grows plants, trees, vines etc., and now Adam and the **adamah** can both grow things.

Adamah is not a living soul but it can grow things (plants, flowers, trees etc.), Adam is a living soul, he has the same power to grow things because he was formed from that growing substance **adamah** but he cannot in his body(earth) grow plants, trees etc. If not what is it that grows in Adam? Man (Adam-Mankind) grows spiritual things. Adam had all that he needed in him; male and female was in him.

God said that Adam needed a helper and He brought every beast and every bird of the air to see what Adam would call them and whatever man called a living thing was what they were but no helper was found for man.

CHAPTER 2-4

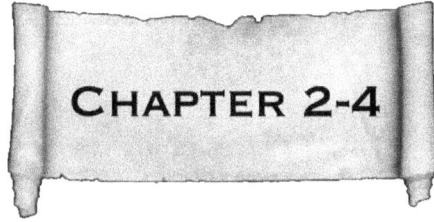

THE FAMILY OF ADAM

Everything that God created serves a purpose in the upkeep and the maintenance of the earth and its natural systems as it relates to plants, trees, animals, insects, fish, birds, the weather, climates, soil, rocks, water etc. and many of them are used as metaphors or similes to explain spiritual truth so that they can be understood in the context that they are presented. As we continue through the Old Testament study we will point out some of these and as you become familiar with them you will begin to notice many more as you read and study.

A **metaphor** is a noun a that is figure of speech in which a term or phrase is applied to something to which it is not literally applicable in order to suggest a resemblance, as in "A mighty fortress is our God" or something used, or regarded as being used, to represent something else; emblem; symbol. A **simile** is a noun that is a figure of speech in which two unlike things are explicitly compared, as in "she is like a rose.", or an instance of such a figure of speech or a use of words exemplifying it.

God planted a garden toward the east in Eden and placed the man there. God is our Father and He is God and He knows where He wants us to be, therefore we can't tell God where we want to go.

God caused trees to grow that were pleasing to the sight and good for food. He included the **tree of life** and the tree of the knowledge of good and evil in the Garden of Eden. He told Adam that he could not eat from the tree of the knowledge of good and evil for the day that he eats of it he would surely die. That means that Adam did not know what evil was. Adam only knew good, because good is God and cannot be defined outside of God, therefore Adam had no knowledge or understanding of evil. Adam had access to the tree of life and he was able to eat of it at will and live forever. This tree is different from the other trees in that is has eternal life as it's fruit.

God specifically mentioned the trees and the different kind of trees in chapter 2. This is where we first learn to understand the metaphor of trees. The tree of life and the tree of the knowledge of good and evil are a clear indication that trees are important and we must consider them in our process of understanding why

God used trees as metaphors or similes. For instance, the tree of life is mentioned and eating from this tree will cause you to live forever.

We now understand that we must pay attention to trees because God uses them to explain some spiritual truths. The **tree of life** is one of those instances. Let's take a look at some of the examples:

As it pertains to wisdom - *She [is] a tree of life to them that lay hold upon her: and happy [is every one] that retaineth her. [Pro 3:18 KJV]*

As it pertains to the fruit, the Hebrew word for fruit is pĕriy [fruit, produce (of the ground fruit, offspring, children, progeny (of the womb) fruit (of actions) (fig.)] of the righteous. Their reward - *The fruit of the righteous [is] a tree of life; and he that winneth souls [is] wise. [Pro 11:30 KJV]*

As it pertains to desire - *Hope deferred maketh the heart sick: but [when] the desire cometh, [it is] a tree of life. [Pro 13:12 KJV]*

As it pertains to a wholesome tongue - *wholesome tongue [is] a tree of life: but perverseness therein [is] a breach in the spirit. [Pro 15:4 KJV]*

The tree of life is mentioned 3 times in the book of Revelation:

- He that hath an ear, let him hear what the Spirit saith unto the churches; To him that overcometh will I give to eat of the tree of life, which is in the midst of the paradise of God. **[Rev 2:7 KJV]**

- In the midst of the street of it, and on either side of the river, [was there] the tree of life, which bare twelve [manner of] fruits, [and] yielded her fruit every month: and the leaves of the tree [were] for the healing of the nations. **[Rev 22:2 KJV]**

- Blessed [are] they that do his commandments, that they may have right to the tree of life, and may enter in through the gates into the city. **[Rev 22:14 KJV]**

Remember no helper was found for Adam. God did not create another Adam, He went inside of Adam took out what was already in him, separated it from him, and made from that rib a man with a womb. Adam was pleased with her and he said that she is now bone of my bone, and flesh of my flesh and he called her woman, womb man. God took the womb out of Adam and gave it back to him. The two of them together are now able to operate as one flesh

And the LORD God caused a deep sleep to fall upon Adam, and he slept: and he took one of his ribs, and closed up the flesh instead thereof; [Gen 2:21 KJV]
And the rib, which the LORD God had taken from man, made he a woman, and brought her unto the man. [Gen 2:22 KJV]

And Adam said, This [is] now bone of my bones, and flesh of my flesh: she shall be called Woman, because she was taken out of Man. [Gen 2:23 KJV]

Therefore shall a man leave his father and his mother, and shall cleave unto his wife: and they shall be one flesh. [Gen 2:24 KJV]

They were naked and knew no shame, they were innocent and they knew no sin. This was the dispensation of innocence. A dispensation is a distinct period in history that forms the framework through which God relates to man. We will mention the ones that are found in the Old Testament the first of which is innocence.

In chapter 3 we find the actions of man changes the dispensation from Innocence to that of Conscience, a time when they become conscience of sin.

The serpent deceived the woman and she presented the opportunity to her husband Adam to sin by convincing him to eat of the fruit of the tree of the knowledge of good and evil, the tree that God told Adam not to eat of. He could eat of any tree but that one. A key to remember in the discussion between the woman and the serpent was the fact that he offered her something that she already had and that was the opportunity to be like God. She was already like God, the deception was to cover up the fact that if she followed his instruction she would actually be like Satan. He was trying to convince her to fix something that was not broken, how can you become what you already are, however, you can become what you are not and that is what happened.

They became what they were not and were no longer living in a state of innocence and now they have the knowledge of good and evil, something they really wanted but now they realize that having it was not as nice as wanting it. Many times that is what happened to us. We do not take the time to consider if what we want is as important as having it, if we did we would never have to return things to stores. Once we arrived at home with it we realized that we really don't like it and return it to the store. You can do that in the natural but it is dangerous to do that in the spirit by deliberately disobeying God because when we do that we get the results of something that we do not want and God already knew that we did not want it and that is why He gave the instructions that were given concerning that situation.

Their act of disobedience to God resulted in them moving to a dispensation of Conscience. We can see what happened at that point Gen 3:22,24 *And the LORD God said, Behold, the man is become as one of us, to know good and evil: and now, lest he put forth his hand, and take also of the tree of life, and eat, and live for ever: [Gen 3:22 KJV]So he drove out the man; and he placed at the east of the garden of Eden Cherubims, and a flaming sword which turned every way, to keep the way of the tree of life. [Gen 3:24 KJV]*

Now man can no longer have access to the tree of life until, Jesus Christ gives up His life so that those that believed on Him and follow Him could return to the state of being in the Garden of Eden and regain access to the tree of life.

Adam and his wife are now living a totally different life than they once knew. They now have a different set of instructions of how they are to live from this point on. One of the first things that we notice was that their eyes were open and they saw that they were naked, they were ashamed to be naked before God and everything else, animals plants etc., they are now listening to Satan because the idea of shame did not come from God, who ask them who told you that you were naked? God already knew the answer to the question that He asked *"And he said, Who told thee that thou [wast] naked? Hast thou eaten of the tree, whereof I commanded thee that thou shouldest not eat? [Gen 3:11 KJV]"*.

In addition to shame, now we see a manifestation of blame, Adam blamed his wife and the woman (womb man) blamed the serpent: "And the man said, *The woman whom thou gavest [to be] with me, she gave me of the tree, and I did eat. [Gen 3:12 KJV]*" Adam tried to improve his position by pointing to the woman, so the LORD directed his attention to the woman *"And the LORD God said unto the woman, What [is] this [that] thou hast done?", then she tried to protect herself by pointing to the serpent, "And the woman said, The serpent beguiled me, and I did eat. [Gen 3:13 KJV]"*. It is interesting to note that neither shame nor blame solve the problem that they faced because of disobedience. The protection that the woman expected from her husband did not happen and now she uses what he used to protect himself to protect herself from the consequences of that bad decision.

The blame still goes on today, there has been much discussion about who sinned, it is believe that Adam is the one who sinned because he had spiritual authority, and some like to say it was the woman because she was the one who listen to the deception of the serpent, but they were not able to avoid the consequences because of the blame game.

Now the LORD speaks to all of them, but He starts with the serpent, "And the LORD God said unto the serpent, Because thou hast done this, ...
  • thou [art] cursed above all cattle, and above every beast of the field;

- upon thy belly shalt thou go, and dust shalt thou eat all the days of thy life: **[Gen 3:14 KJV]**"

The serpent received a curse that changed the way it lived, and God also pronounced something metaphorically that addressed the future relationship between the serpent (Satan was speaking through the serpent) Christ, His woman (bride) and Satan. God continued to say "And …

- *I will put enmity between thee and the woman,*
- *and between thy seed and her seed;*
- *it shall bruise thy head, and thou shalt bruise his heel. [Gen 3:15 KJV]*

Satan used the serpent to deceive and he is still using deception as one of his tools to get us to follow him.

Next God addressed what the woman consequences are and said *"Unto the woman he said,*

- *I will greatly multiply thy sorrow and thy conception;*
- *in sorrow thou shalt bring forth children;*
- *and thy desire [shall be] to thy husband,*
- *and he shall rule over thee. [Gen 3:16 KJV]"*

Finally God said to Adam *"And unto Adam he said, Because thou hast hearkened unto the voice of thy wife, and hast eaten of the tree, of which I commanded thee, saying, Thou shalt not eat of it: ….."*

- *cursed [is] the ground for thy sake; in sorrow shalt thou eat [of] it all the days of thy life; [Gen 3:17 KJV]*
- *Thorns also and thistles shall it bring forth to thee; and thou shalt eat the herb of the field; [Gen 3:18 KJV]*
- *In the sweat of thy face shalt thou eat bread, till thou return unto the ground; for out of it wast thou taken: for dust thou [art], and unto dust shalt thou return. [Gen 3:19 KJV]*

God gave all of them instructions changing the way and the order of their existence would be from this point on.

And Adam called his wife's name Eve; because she was the mother of all living. **[Gen 3:20 KJV]**. This is also interesting, because the Bible did not say how they did it but they were obeying God and reproducing themselves in the earth prior to this event, but under this new order the woman is now the mother of all living. This is the first time that mother is mentioned; they were reproducing differently than the animals before this time. We know that the animals were giving birth after their own kind and so was Adam, which is proven by the people that were on the earth when Cain had to leave the family. He was afraid of the people and he also found women as wives already on the planet.

After the new instructions God covered them with animal skins, they had covered themselves with fig tree leaves, but God knew that it would take blood to cover them and He used animal skin, later on we will notice that the blood of animals was used to establish a relationship with God with His people, "Unto Adam also and to his wife did the LORD God make coats of skins, and clothed them. **[Gen 3:21 KJV]**"

Adam and his wife gave birth to two sons after this, Cain and Able. This was the beginning of two different blood lines in the earth. One would have a heart for God and follow Him the other would follow his own heart which was connected with the world system that Satan in now in control of.

Cain and Able brought a sacrifice to God. Able's sacrifice was accepted by God but Cain's was not. God did tell Cain that He would accept him if he did well, but Cain did not want to do well he wanted God to accept his offering under his conditions and God will not do that. Cain was not happy about having to do well so he decided to kill his brother as if that would eliminate his need to do well.

This is a great lesson for us because no matter how wrong we are treated we cannot get God to change His order just because we are hurt, misused or abused by people. We are the ones that have to change. The encounter that Cain had with God is clear, but the reality of Cain's bad choice was not clear to him until after he did what he thought was best to do. The account of what happened is as follows:

- *But unto Cain and to his offering he had not respect. And Cain was very wroth, and his countenance fell. [Gen 4:5 KJV]*

- *And the LORD said unto Cain, Why art thou wroth? and why is thy countenance fallen? [Gen 4:6 KJV]*

- *If thou doest well, shalt thou not be accepted? and if thou doest not well, sin lieth at the door. And unto thee [shall be] his desire, and thou shalt rule over him. [Gen 4:7 KJV]*

This is the last time that the life of Cain is followed in the Old Testament. He chose to follow the world system. Cain and his family begin to follow a path that was totally different from the people of God.

Cain decided that he did not want to obey God and therefore was banned from God's face and the earth would no longer yield to him.

And now [art] thou cursed from the earth, which hath opened her mouth to receive thy brother's blood from thy hand; [Gen 4:11 KJV]

When thou tillest the ground, it shall not henceforth yield unto thee her strength; a fugitive and a vagabond shalt thou be in the earth. [Gen 4:12 KJV]

And Cain said unto the LORD, My punishment [is] greater than I can bear. [Gen 4:13 KJV] – <u>Cain cannot bear to have happen to him what he did to his brother.</u>

Behold, thou hast driven me out this day from the face of the earth; and from thy face shall I be hid; and I shall be a fugitive and a vagabond in the earth; and it shall come to pass, [that] every one that findeth me shall slay me. [Gen 4:14 KJV] – <u>Where did these people come from since the Bible only mentions Adam, Eve, Abel and Cain by name? One of God's commandments was to multiply and they must have obeyed God. How many people did Cain think would slay him? Cain said everyone that find me shall slay me.</u>

It is important that we understand the nature of sin and the opportunity that presents itself to pass down through family bloodlines as it did in Cain's blood line. Cain would not repent of killing his brother and therefore murder became an iniquity and a generational curse in his family bloodline.

The LORD put a mark upon Cain to protect him and he went out from the presence of the LORD and dwelled in the land of Nob on the east of Eden, he married and begins to have children. His decedents begin to do other things and invent other things and they are the ones mentioned as having done some things for the first time in history.

One of Cain's children was the one who inherited the generational curse that was mentioned previously. Many times when we do things we think that it is only going to hurt us so we do not repent and break that issue in our lives. When we do that we position that issue in our bloodline to be inherited by one or more of our children and their children and so on until someone is bold enough to break it from themselves and the bloodline.

Take a look at what happened to Cain:

Note: The number Seven is a symbol of completeness, perfection good or evil. Look for the symbolism in the numbers that God uses and you will be able to follow His thought process as you study.

And the LORD said unto him, Therefore whosoever slayeth Cain, vengeance shall be taken on him sevenfold. And the LORD set a mark upon Cain, lest any finding him should kill him. [Gen 4:15 KJV] <u>God put the fear of God in the people so that they would not kill Cain, this comforted</u> *Cain and he And Cain went out from the presence of the LORD, and dwelt in the land of Nod, on the east of Eden. [Gen 4:16 KJV]* – Cain and his wife had a son Enoch, the genealogy of his bloodline and the works of their hands is mentioned in Genesis chapter 4.

They begin to build and invent things. Cain built a city and names it after his son, his descendants begin to do things in the earth related to the natural part of the earth, the world system that Satan now has control over. Sin grows in his family line by leaps and bounds.

Cain and his father Adam had only one wife, **but Cain's decendent Lamech four generations later took for himself two wives, he was the one that you can most notice the operation of the generational curse.**

Not only did he have two wives, he murdered two men and then believed that God would protect him from being murdered just as God had protected Cain, his great, great, great, great grandfather four generations before him. We see the account of that in the following passage: *And Lamech said unto his wives, Adah and Zillah, Hear my voice; ye wives of Lamech, hearken unto my speech: for I have slain a man to my wounding, and a young man to my hurt. [Gen 4:23 KJV]. If Cain shall be avenged sevenfold, truly Lamech seventy and sevenfold. [Gen 4:24 KJV]*

Here is an interesting statement by Lamech, he expected to be forgiven seventy and sevenfold and we can follow this in the New Testament when Peter asked Jesus how many times should he forgive his brother seven times? Then Jesus replied and said *"Jesus saith unto him, I say not unto thee, Until seven times: but, Until seventy times seven. [Mat 18:22 KJV]"* God had originally said to Cain sevenfold, this is important to note. As you study the Old Testament you should be able to recognize instances where you can see the beginning of something that you believe and follow that so that you can better recognized the difference between good and evil and not just right from wrong.

Cain's descendants were responsible for the following inventions:

- First time tent dwellers and cattlemen - *And Adah bare Jabal: he was the father of such as dwell in tents, and [of such as have] cattle. [Gen 4:20 KJV]*

- Musical instrument harp and organ - *And his brother's name [was] Jubal: he was the father of all such as handle the harp and organ. [Gen 4:21 KJV]*
- Every artificer in brass and iron - *And Zillah, she also bare Tubalcain, an instructer of every artificer in brass and iron: and the sister of Tubalcain [was] Naamah. [Gen 4:22 KJV]*

For more information see Holman Book of Biblical Charts, Maps and Reconstructions.

Cain's bloodline (genealogy) is not mentioned any more specifically to him, he blended into the people of the land and is no longer specifically mentioned as to the following his descendants down through history in biblical events and happenings. His story is told in world history because these are the people that were making world history up until the time of Noah.

CHAPTER 5

THE GENEALOGY OF THE PEOPLE FROM ADAM VIA (SETH)

And Adam knew his wife again; and she bare a son, and called his name Seth: For God, [said she], hath appointed me another seed instead of Abel, whom Cain slew. [Gen 4:25 KJV]. And to Seth, to him also there was born a son; and he called his name Enos: then began men to call upon the name of the LORD. [Gen 4:26 KJV]

Now we see the genealogy of Adam via Seth and this is the blood line that God will use to pass down the holy seed (**this is the seed that God talk to the serpent about, the one that He would eventually bring into the earth, God said, I will put enmity between thee and the woman, and between thy seed and her seed**) that seed being the person of Jesus Christ. Each person that was born that specifically carried the holy seed is mentioned by name in the genealogy of Adam via Seth. There were many people mentioned that were born of that particular person, but the one that carried the seed is the only one mentioned by name. We see that in chapter 5

This [is] the book of the generations of Adam. In the day that God created man, in the likeness of God made he him; **[Gen 5:1 KJV]**

Male and female created he them; and blessed them, **and called their name Adam**, in the day when they were created. **[Gen 5:2 KJV]**

And Adam lived an hundred and thirty years, and begat [a son] in **his own likeness**, after his image; and called his name **Seth**: **[Gen 5:3 KJV]**

And the days of Adam after he had begotten Seth were eight hundred years: and he begat sons and daughters: **[Gen 5:4 KJV]**. This is interesting because Cain was the biological son of Adam but he did not display the likeness of Adam, or the image of Adam which was connected to and came from God.

And all the days that Adam lived were nine hundred and thirty years: and he died. **[Gen 5:5 KJV]**

And Seth lived an hundred and five years, and begat **Enos**: **[Gen 5:6 KJV]**
And Seth lived after he begat Enos eight hundred and seven years, and begat sons and daughters: **[Gen 5:7 KJV]**

And all the days of Seth were nine hundred and twelve years: and he died. **[Gen 5:8 KJV]**

And Enos lived ninety years, and begat **Cainan**: **[Gen 5:9 KJV]**

And Enos lived after he begat Cainan eight hundred and fifteen years, and begat sons and daughters: **[Gen 5:10 KJV]**

And all the days of Enos were nine hundred and five years: and he died. [Gen 5:11 KJV]

And Cainan lived seventy years, and begat **Mahalaleel**: **[Gen 5:12 KJV]**

And Cainan lived after he begat Mahalaleel eight hundred and forty years, and begat sons and daughters: **[Gen 5:13 KJV]**

And all the days of Cainan were nine hundred and ten years: and he died. **[Gen 5:14 KJV]**

And Mahalaleel lived sixty and five years, and begat **Jared**: **[Gen 5:15 KJV]**

And Mahalaleel lived after he begat Jared eight hundred and thirty years, and begat sons and daughters: **[Gen 5:16 KJV]**

And all the days of Mahalaleel were eight hundred ninety and five years: and he died. [Gen 5:17 KJV]

And Jared lived an hundred sixty and two years, and he begat **Enoch**: **[Gen 5:18 KJV]**

And Jared lived after he begat Enoch eight hundred years, and begat sons and daughters: **[Gen 5:19 KJV]**

And all the days of Jared were nine hundred sixty and two years: and he died. **[Gen 5:20 KJV]**

And Enoch lived sixty and five years, and begat **Methuselah**: **[Gen 5:21 KJV]**

And Enoch walked with God after he begat Methuselah three hundred years, and begat sons and daughters: **[Gen 5:22 KJV]**

And all the days of Enoch were three hundred sixty and five years: **[Gen 5:23 KJV]**

And Enoch walked with God: and he [was] not; for God took him. **[Gen 5:24 KJV]**

And Methuselah lived an hundred eighty and seven years, and begat **Lamech**: **[Gen 5:25 KJV]**

And Methuselah lived after he begat Lamech seven hundred eighty and two years, and begat sons and daughters: **[Gen 5:26 KJV]**

And all the days of Methuselah were nine hundred sixty and nine years: and he died. **[Gen 5:27 KJV]**

And Lamech lived an hundred eighty and two years, and begat a son: **[Gen 5:28 KJV]**

And he called his name **Noah**, saying, This [same] shall comfort us concerning our work and toil of our hands, because of the ground which the LORD hath cursed. **[Gen 5:29 KJV]**

And Lamech lived after he begat Noah five hundred ninety and five years, and begat sons and daughters: **[Gen 5:30 KJV]**

And all the days of Lamech were seven hundred seventy and seven years: and he died. **[Gen 5:31 KJV]**

And Noah was five hundred years old: and Noah begat Shem, Ham, and Japheth. **[Gen 5:32 KJV]**

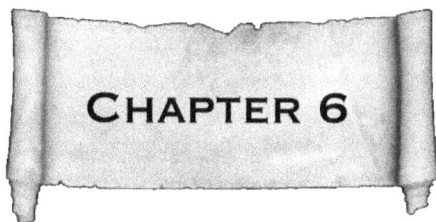

CHAPTER 6

NOAH'S FAMILY

God Judges the wickedness of the Earth

- Chapter 6 – God Establishes His Covenant with Noah – **Dispensation of Government – Noah is the head of God's system during this dispensation**

- Men begin to multiply on the earth and daughters were born - *And it came to pass, when men began to multiply on the face of the earth, and daughters were born unto them, [Gen 6:1 KJV]*

- Sons of God saw that the daughters of men were fair to look upon and they took them wives as they choose - *That the sons of God saw the daughters of men that they [were] fair; and they took them wives of all which they chose. [Gen 6:2 KJV]*

- God limits man years to 120 - *And the LORD said, My spirit shall not always strive with man, for that he also [is] flesh: yet his days shall be an hundred and twenty years. [Gen 6:3 KJV]*

- The wickedness of man grieved God - *And GOD saw that the wickedness of man [was] great in the earth, and [that] every imagination of the thoughts of his heart [was] only evil continually. [Gen 6:5 KJV] And it repented the LORD that he had made man on the earth, and it grieved him at his heart. [Gen 6:6 KJV]And the LORD said, I will destroy man whom I have created from the face of the earth; both man, and beast, and the creeping thing, and the fowls of the air; for it repenteth me that I have made them. [Gen 6:7 KJV]*

- **God decided to start over with Noah, God was grieved but he found one just man and that was enough for him to start over without destroying all** - *But Noah found grace in the eyes of the LORD. [Gen 6:8 KJV]* Later in chapter 7 we will see where God said that Noah was righteous before him just as he said about Abraham. This reminds us of when **Abraham was pleading with God to save Sodom and Gomorrah for the sake of ten righteous men** - *And he said, Oh let not the Lord be angry, and I will speak yet but this once: Peradventure ten shall be found there. And he said, I will not destroy [it] for ten's sake. [Gen 18:32 KJV] and then when God gave his only begotten son to save the whole world. For God so loved the world, that he gave his only begotten Son, that whosoever believeth in him should not perish, but have everlasting life. [Jhn 3:16 KJV]*

If we had paid attention to what the LORD did with Noah we would realize that God was willing to start over with only one man.

- God finds Noah a just man and perfect in his generations - *These [are] the generations of Noah: Noah was a just man [and] perfect in his generations, [and] Noah walked with God. [Gen 6:9 KJV] And Noah begat three sons, Shem, Ham, and Japheth. [Gen 6:10 KJV] The earth also was corrupt before God, and the earth was filled with violence. [Gen 6:11 KJV]*

- God is going to destroy all flesh with the breath of life - *Make thee an ark of gopher wood; rooms shalt thou make in the ark, and shalt pitch it within and without with pitch. [Gen 6:14 KJV] And, behold, I, even I, do bring a flood of waters upon the earth, to destroy all flesh, wherein [is] the breath of life, from under heaven; [and] every thing that [is] in the earth shall die. [Gen 6:17 KJV]*

God established a covenant with Noah and gives him information of the coming flood and instructions to prepare for it. Noah had never seen rain so this is going to be a faith walk with God. Noah believed what God said - *But with thee will I establish my covenant; and thou shalt come into the ark, thou, and thy sons, and thy wife, and thy sons' wives with thee. [Gen 6:18 KJV] And of every living thing of all flesh, two of every [sort] shalt thou bring into the ark, to keep [them] alive with thee; they shall be male and female. [Gen 6:19 KJV] Of fowls after their kind, and of cattle after their kind, of every creeping thing of the earth after his kind, two of every [sort] shall come unto thee, to keep [them] alive. [Gen 6:20 KJV] And take thou unto thee of all food that is eaten, and thou shalt gather [it] to thee; and it shall be for food for thee, and for them. [Gen 6:21 KJV] Thus did Noah; according to all that God commanded him, so did he. [Gen 6:22 KJV]*

CHAPTER 7

THE TIME OF THE FLOOD HAD COME

- God commanded Noah to go into the ark with his family and to take all of the animals that He commanded him to take and Noah did as God had command him - *Of every clean beast thou shalt take to thee by sevens, the male and his female: and of beasts that [are] not clean by two, the male and his female. [Gen 7:2 KJV] Of fowls also of the air by sevens, the male and the female; to keep seed alive upon the face of all the earth. [Gen 7:3 KJV] For yet seven days, and I will cause it to rain upon the earth forty days and forty nights; and every living substance that I have made will I destroy from off the face of the earth. [Gen 7:4 KJV] And Noah did according unto all that the LORD commanded him. [Gen 7:5 KJV]*

- After one hundred years of building the ark it was time for the rain. *Noah did all the LORD had commanded him to do - And Noah did according unto all that the LORD commanded him. [Gen 7:5 KJV] In the six hundredth year of Noah's life, in the second month, the seventeenth day of the month, the same day were all the fountains of the great deep broken up, and the windows of heaven were opened. [Gen 7:11 KJV] And the rain was upon the earth forty days and forty nights. [Gen 7:12 KJV] In the selfsame day entered Noah, and Shem, and Ham, and Japheth, the sons of Noah, and Noah's wife, and the three wives of his sons with them, into the ark; [Gen 7:13 KJV]*

- The flood drowned everything that had breath and God has started over with Noah. The water prevailed upon the earth for one hundred and fifty days and the only ones that remained alive were the ones in the arc with Noah - *And all flesh died that moved upon the earth, both of fowl, and of cattle, and of beast, and of every creeping thing that creepeth upon the earth, and every man: [Gen 7:21 KJV] All in whose nostrils [was] the breath of life, of all that [was] in the dry [land], died. [Gen 7:22 KJV] And every living substance was destroyed which was upon the face of the ground, both man, and cattle, and the creeping things, and the fowl of the heaven; and they were destroyed from the earth: and Noah only remained [alive], and they that [were] with him in the ark. [Gen 7:23 KJV]And the waters prevailed upon the earth an hundred and fifty days [Gen 7:24 KJV]*

CHAPTER 8

THE FLOOD IS OVER THE EARTH IS DRIED

- The rain stops the water subsides and the flood is over and God is ready to release them from the arc. - *And God remembered Noah, and every living thing, and all the cattle that [was] with him in the ark: and God made a wind to pass over the earth, and the waters asswaged; [Gen 8:1 KJV]The fountains also of the deep and the windows of heaven were stopped, and the rain from heaven was restrained; [Gen 8:2 KJV]And the waters returned from off the earth continually: and after the end of the hundred and fifty days the waters were abated. [Gen 8:3 KJV] And the ark rested in the seventh month, on the seventeenth day of the month, upon the mountains of Ararat. [Gen 8:4 KJV] And in the second month, on the seven and twentieth day of the month, was the earth dried. [Gen 8:14 KJV]*

- God speaks to Noah and tell him to leave the arc and go back to the dry land and release everything that was in the arc with him - *And God spake unto Noah, saying, [Gen 8:15 KJV] Go forth of the ark, thou, and thy wife, and thy sons, and thy sons' wives with thee. [Gen 8:16 KJV] Bring forth with thee every living thing that [is] with thee, of all flesh, [both] of fowl, and of cattle, and of every creeping thing that creepeth upon the earth; that they may breed abundantly in the earth, and be fruitful, and multiply upon the earth. [Gen 8:17 KJV] And Noah went forth, and his sons, and his wife, and his sons' wives with him: [Gen 8:18 KJV] Every beast, every creeping thing, and every fowl, [and] whatsoever creepeth upon the earth, after their kinds, went forth out of the ark. [Gen 8:19 KJV]*

- Noah built an alter and offered offerings before the LORD and the LORD was please and said in His heart that He would never curse the earth again for man's sake, nor would he smite any more every living thing as He had done. - *And Noah builded an altar unto the LORD; and took of every clean beast, and of every clean fowl, and offered burnt offerings on the altar. [Gen 8:20 KJV] And the LORD smelled a sweet savour; and the LORD said in his heart, I will not again curse the ground any more for man's sake; for the imagination of man's heart [is] evil from his youth; neither will I again smite any more every thing living, as I have done. [Gen 8:21 KJV]*

This is very important to remember – the word God gave to Noah was that while the earth remained there would always be seedtime and harvest, cold and heat, summer and winter and day and night will not cease. *While the earth remaineth, seedtime and harvest, and cold and heat, and summer and winter, and day and night shall not cease. [Gen 8:22 KJV]*

As we move on from this point we must keep up with the holy seed and it is now traveling down through the bloodline of Sem the son of Noah – As we see in the genealogy of Jesus as found in Luke chapter 3 - *Which was [the son] of Cainan, which was [the son] of Arphaxad, which was [the son] of Sem, which was [the son] of Noe, which was [the son] of Lamech, [Luk 3:36 KJV]*

CHAPTER 9

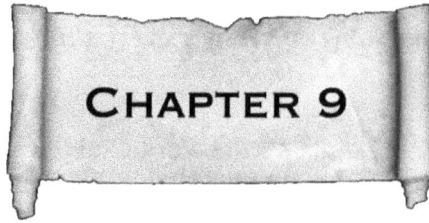

GOD GIVES NOAH GOVERNMENTAL AUTHORITY OVER THE PLANET

- God confirms His covenant with Noah and includes everything that is with Noah as a part of the covenant and God blessed Noah and his sons and gave them the instructions of the covenant.

However, there is a slight difference in what God commanded Noah to do from what God had given Adam to do. Notice the differences:

God told Noah to - Be fruitful, and multiply, and replenish the earth. [Gen 9:1 KJV]. <u>**Notice that he was not told to subdue it: and have dominion.**</u> Now we have to wait for Jesus to die on the cross to regain the ability to subdue and have dominion as Adam once had before he gave it to Satan. Jesus had to pay the price for us to get that back, He did and now we can subdue and have dominion.

God told Noah that those that Adam was told to subdue and have dominion over are now **to fear you and a dread of you shall be upon them** - *And the fear of you and the dread of you shall be upon every beast of the earth, and upon every fowl of the air, upon all that moveth [upon] the earth, and upon all the fishes of the sea; into your hand are they delivered. [Gen 9:2 KJV]*

God told Noah that the food for him includes things that Adam was not given permission to eat. Noah can now eat every moving thing that lives on the earth as well as the green herbs - Every moving thing that liveth shall be meat for you; even as the green herb have I given you all things. *[Gen 9:3 KJV] But flesh with the life thereof, [which is] the blood thereof, shall ye not eat. [Gen 9:4 KJV] And surely your blood of your lives will I require; at the hand of every beast will I require it, and at the hand of man; at the hand of every man's brother will I require the life of man. [Gen 9:5 KJV] Adam was given permission before sin to eat from the trees in the garden and after sin to eat - ..... and thou shalt eat the herb of the field; [Gen 3:18 KJV] In the sweat of thy face shalt thou eat bread, ...*

God spoke again to Noah and his sons about covenant and that He would set a bow in the sky as a sign of His covenant - *And I will establish my covenant with you; neither shall all flesh be cut off any more by the waters of a flood; neither shall there any more be a flood to destroy the earth. [Gen 9:11 KJV] And God said, This [is] the token of the covenant which I make between me and you and every living creature that [is] with you, for perpetual generations: [Gen 9:12 KJV] I do set my bow in the cloud, and it shall be for a token of a covenant between me and the earth. [Gen 9:13 KJV] And it shall come to pass, when I bring a cloud over the earth, that the bow shall be seen in the cloud: [Gen 9:14 KJV] And I will remember my covenant, which [is] between me and you and every living creature of all flesh; and the waters shall no more become a flood to destroy all flesh. [Gen 9:15 KJV]*

Noah was the spiritual authority in the earth. He was the gatekeeper; whatever he said to be done God was going to back him up because he was the one managing the earth at that time. Noah's three sons were to repopulate the earth, Noah was the governing authority, but one of his sons did not honor that authority and was cursed by his father for the dishonor and disrespect. Noah was wrong, he got drunk from wine that he made but he was still the person that God had left in charge of the planet.

You do not get to override God's order or His delegated authority. *These [are] the three sons of Noah: and of them was the whole earth overspread. [Gen 9:19 KJV] And Noah began [to be] an husbandman, and he planted a vineyard: [Gen 9:20 KJV] And Ham, the father of Canaan, saw the nakedness of his father, and told his two brethren without. [Gen 9:22 KJV] And Noah awoke from his wine, and knew what his younger son had done unto him. [Gen 9:24 KJV] And he said, Cursed [be] Canaan; a servant of servants shall he be unto his brethren. [Gen 9:25 KJV] And he said, Blessed [be] the LORD God of Shem; and Canaan shall be his servant. [Gen 9:26 KJV] God shall enlarge Japheth, and he shall dwell in the tents of Shem; and Canaan shall be his servant. [Gen 9:27 KJV]*

CHAPTER 10

THE GENEALOGY OF THE SPREADING OF NOAH'S SONS OVER ALL OF THE EARTH

There is much debate of how the earth was populated by Noah's sons about what race of people came from which son but there are maps that indicate what nation was born in what territory. This is the account of the generations of Noah's family and the territory that they occupied:

Now these [are] the generations of the sons of Noah, Shem, Ham, and Japheth: and unto them were sons born after the flood. [Gen 10:1 KJV] The sons of Japheth; Gomer, and Magog, and Madai, and Javan, and Tubal, and Meshech, and Tiras. [Gen 10:2 KJV] And the sons of Gomer; Ashkenaz, and Riphath, and Togarmah. [Gen 10:3 KJV] And the sons of Javan; Elishah, and Tarshish, Kittim, and Dodanim. [Gen 10:4 KJV] By these were the isles of the Gentiles divided in their lands; every one after his tongue, after their families, in their nations. [Gen 10:5 KJV] And the sons of Ham; Cush, and Mizraim, and Phut, and Canaan. [Gen 10:6 KJV] And the sons of Cush; Seba, and Havilah, and Sabtah, and Raamah, and Sabtecha: and the sons of Raamah; Sheba, and Dedan. [Gen 10:7 KJV] And Cush begat Nimrod: he began to be a mighty one in the earth. [Gen 10:8 KJV] He was a mighty hunter before the LORD: wherefore it is said, <u>Even as Nimrod the mighty hunter before the LORD. [Gen 10:9 KJV] And the beginning of his kingdom was Babel, and Erech, and Accad, and Calneh, in the land of Shinar.</u> [Gen 10:10 KJV] And the Hivite, and the Arkite, and the Sinite, [Gen 10:17 KJV] And the Arvadite, and the Zemarite, and the Hamathite: and afterward were the families of the Canaanites spread abroad. [Gen 10:18 KJV] And the border of the Canaanites was from Sidon, as thou comest to Gerar, unto Gaza; as thou goest, unto Sodom, and Gomorrah, and Admah, and Zeboim, even unto Lasha. [Gen 10:19 KJV]These [are] the sons of Ham, after their families, after their tongues, in their countries, [and] in their nations. [Gen 10:20 KJV] Unto Shem also, the father of all the children of Eber, the brother of Japheth the elder, even to him were [children] born. [Gen 10:21 KJV] The children of Shem; Elam, and Asshur, and Arphaxad, and Lud, and Aram. [Gen 10:22 KJV] And the children of Aram; Uz, and Hul, and Gether, and Mash. [Gen 10:23 KJV] And unto Eber were born two sons: the name of one [was] Peleg; for in his days was the earth divided; and his brother's name [was] Joktan.

[Gen 10:25 KJV] And Joktan begat Almodad, and Sheleph, and Hazarmaveth, and Jerah, [Gen 10:26 KJV] And Hadoram, and Uzal, and Diklah, [Gen 10:27 KJV] And Obal, and Abimael, and Sheba, [Gen 10:28 KJV] And Ophir, and Havilah, and Jobab: all these [were] the sons of Joktan. [Gen 10:29 KJV] And their dwelling was from Mesha, as thou goest unto Sephar a mount of the east. [Gen 10:30 KJV] These [are] the sons of Shem, after their families, after their tongues, in their lands, after their nations. [Gen 10:31 KJV] These [are] the families of the sons of Noah, after their generations, in their nations: and by these were the nations divided in the earth after the flood. [Gen 10:32 KJV]

CHAPTER 11

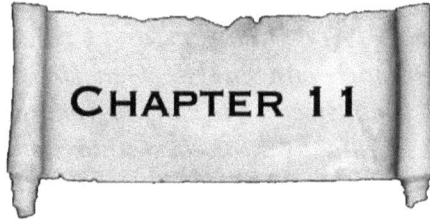

THE EARTH SPOKE ONE LANGUAGE / ABRAM FAMILY STORY BEGINS

- They decided to build a city and tower whose top would reach heaven. They were all on one accord and they all wanted to stay together they did not want to be scattered.

And the whole earth was of one language, and of one speech. [Gen 11:1 KJV] And it came to pass, as they journeyed from the east, that they found a plain in the land of Shinar; and they dwelt there. [Gen 11:2 KJV] And they said one to another, Go to, let us make brick, and burn them throughly. And they had brick for stone, and slime had they for morter. [Gen 11:3 KJV] And they said, Go to, let us build us a city and a tower, whose top [may reach] unto heaven; and let us make us a name, lest we be scattered abroad upon the face of the whole earth. [Gen 11:4 KJV]

- God had given Noah the command to replenish the earth and they had decided that they did not want to do that and they were all on one accord in their decision. They were operating as one man and the LORD came down to see the city and the tower that the children of men were building. God said that the people is one indicating one man and that they all had one language and because of this nothing would be restrained from them. This lets us know that when we all agree and are all of one accord there is nothing that is restrained from us.

And the LORD came down to see the city and the tower, which the children of men builded. [Gen 11:5 KJV] And the LORD said Behold, the people [is] one, and they have all one language; and this they begin to do: and now nothing will be restrained from them, which they have imagined to do. [Gen 11:6 KJV]

- God came down and confound their language so that they would not understand each other and scatter them abroad from upon the earth. Now they are going to repopulate the earth as God had originally spoken. Notice that God did not rebuke them, nor was He angry with them. They were using a spiritual law that God wants us to use today, but they were using it for the wrong reason and God gave them some correction and help to get going in the correct direction.

Go to, let us go down, and there confound their language, that they may not understand one another's speech. [Gen 11:7 KJV] So the LORD scattered them abroad from thence upon the face of all the earth: and they left off to build the city. [Gen 11:8 KJV] Therefore is the name of it called Babel; because the LORD did there confound the language of all the earth: and from thence did the LORD scatter them abroad upon the face of all the earth. [Gen 11:9 KJV]

- Speaking one language is very important; we still struggle with communications problems even if we speak the same language. God does intend for us to speak one language again and when we do that and become on one accord with each other and with Holy Spirit. There is nothing that we can imagine to do that we cannot do. God gave one language back to us on the day of Pentecost. It is through and by Holy Spirit that we are able to speak in a language that we have no knowledge of. They all received Holy Spirit with the evidence of speaking in tongues. *Now when this was noised abroad, the multitude came together, and were confounded, because that every man heard them speak in his own language. [Act 2:6 KJV] And they were all amazed and marvelled, saying one to another, Behold, are not all these which speak Galilaeans? [Act 2:7 KJV] And how hear we every man in our own tongue, wherein we were born? [Act 2:8 KJV]*

- Now that God has set everything back in order and continues with the bloodline of the holy seed via the bloodline of Shem. God keeps taking us back to the genealogies because He wants to make sure that we understand that He must be able to trace everyone back to him that belongs to him. Shem is from the line of ancestors of Abram later known as Abraham and we can see how God continued this genealogy that he started with Adam through Seth all the way down to Abram/Abraham.

These [are] the generations of Shem: Shem [was] an hundred years old, and begat Arphaxad two years after the flood: [Gen 11:10 KJV] And Shem lived after he begat Arphaxad five hundred years, and begat sons and daughters. [Gen 11:11 KJV] And Arphaxad lived five and thirty years, and begat Salah: [Gen 11:12 KJV] And Arphaxad lived after he begat Salah four hundred and three years, and begat sons and daughters. [Gen 11:13 KJV] And Salah lived thirty years, and begat Eber: [Gen 11:14 KJV] And Salah lived after he begat Eber four hundred and three years, and begat sons and daughters. [Gen 11:15 KJV] And Eber lived four and thirty years, and begat Peleg: [Gen 11:16 KJV] And Eber lived after he begat Peleg four hundred and thirty years, and begat sons and daughters. [Gen 11:17 KJV] And Peleg lived thirty years, and begat Reu: [Gen 11:18 KJV] And Peleg lived after he begat Reu two hundred and nine years, and begat sons and daughters. [Gen 11:19 KJV] And Reu lived two and thirty years, and begat Serug: [Gen 11:20 KJV] And Reu lived after he begat Serug two hundred and seven years, and begat sons and daughters. [Gen 11:21 KJV]And Serug lived thirty years, and begat Nahor: [Gen 11:22 KJV]And Serug lived after he begat Nahor two hundred years, and begat sons and daughters. [Gen 11:23 KJV]And Nahor lived nine and twenty years, and begat Terah: [Gen 11:24 KJV]And Nahor lived after he begat Terah an hundred and nineteen years, and begat sons and daughters. [Gen 11:25 KJV]And Terah lived seventy years, and begat Abram, Nahor, and Haran. [Gen 11:26 KJV]

❖ Now we see the beginning of Abrams family, specifically his father Terah, and it is interesting that Terah was on his way to Canaan, the land that God would eventually lead Abram to and give to him as an inheritance for his seed. Terah stopped in Haran and never made it to Canaan. The Bible does not give the reason that Terah was on his way to Canaan but it does say that is where he was headed and that he was taking all of his family with him.

Now these [are] the generations of Terah: Terah begat Abram, Nahor, and Haran; and Haran begat Lot. [Gen 11:27 KJV] And Haran died before his father Terah in the land of his nativity, in Ur of the Chaldees. [Gen 11:28 KJV] And Abram and Nahor took them wives: the name of Abram's wife [was] Sarai; and the name of Nahor's wife, Milcah, the daughter of Haran, the father of Milcah, and the father of Iscah. [Gen 11:29 KJV]But Sarai was barren; she [had] no child. [Gen 11:30 KJV]And Terah took Abram his son, and Lot the son of Haran his son's son, and Sarai his daughter in law, his son Abram's wife; and they went forth with them from Ur of the Chaldees, to go into the land of Canaan; and they came unto Haran, and dwelt there. [Gen 11:31 KJV]And the days of Terah were two hundred and five years: and Terah died in Haran. [Gen 11:32 KJV]

After the death of Terah, the father of Abram, God speaks to Abram in the beginning of chapter 12

CHAPTER 12

ABRAM-ABRAHAM THE DISPENSATION OF PROMISE

❖ God calls Abram out from his family and sends him forth

God calls Abram and made some promises to him. Abram at this point does not even question who this God is and where is it that he is sending him. When he understood what God was asking him to do he did it without question. This indicates that he must have been an obedient son to his natural father. Not many people will obey people that they are supposed to obey in this day and time, but I can imagine it must have taken some level of trust to obey God as Abram did. While he trusted God to leave his father's house, he did have a challenge trusting God to protect him from the natives of the land that he would travel trough.

Now the LORD had said unto Abram, Get thee out of thy country, and from thy kindred, and from thy father's house, unto a land that I will shew thee: [Gen 12:1 KJV] And I will make of thee a great nation, and I will bless thee, and make thy name great; and thou shalt be a blessing: [Gen 12:2 KJV] And I will bless them that bless thee, and curse him that curseth thee: and in thee shall all families of the earth be blessed. [Gen 12:3 KJV] So Abram departed, as the LORD had spoken unto him; and Lot went with him: and Abram [was] seventy and five years old when he departed out of Haran. [Gen 12:4 KJV]

Abram took his wife and Lot his brother's son and headed south. He was willing to obey God to leave his family but he was still afraid of the inhabitants of the lands that he would have to travel through. As he traveled through the land God spoke to him about giving him the land and to his seed and Abram built an altar at Bethel and **called upon the name of the LORD =Jehovah = "the existing One."**

Notice that Abram called upon the name of the LORD. Just calling upon the name of the LORD get results in the earth. Remember, this was before we read *That at the name of Jesus every knee should bow, of [things] in heaven, and [things] in earth, and [things] under the earth; [Phl 2:10 KJV]*

And Abram took Sarai his wife, and Lot his brother's son, and all their substance that they had gathered, and the souls that they had gotten in Haran;

and they went forth to go into the land of Canaan; and into the land of Canaan they came. [Gen 12:5 KJV]And Abram passed through the land unto the place of Sichem, unto the plain of Moreh. And the Canaanite [was] then in the land. [Gen 12:6 KJV]And the LORD appeared unto Abram, and said, Unto thy seed will I give this land: and there builded he an altar unto the LORD, who appeared unto him. [Gen 12:7 KJV] And he removed from thence unto a mountain on the east of Bethel, and pitched his tent, [having] Bethel on the west, and Hai on the east: and there he builded an altar unto the LORD, and called upon the name of the LORD. [Gen 12:8 KJV] And Abram journeyed, going on still toward the south. [Gen 12:9 KJV]

As they passed through Egypt Abram asked his wife to pretend that she was his sister because they may want to kill him to take her because of her beauty, she agreed and was taken by Pharaoh, but God protected her and did honor what He had previously told him … *I will bless them that bless thee, and curse him that curseth thee: and in thee shall all families of the earth be blessed. [Gen 12:3 KJV]* and that is what happened, God cursed Pharaoh and plagued his house because of Sarai, Abram's wife. Perhaps he did not remember what God said, because he did the same thing later on another occasion.

Therefore it shall come to pass, when the Egyptians shall see thee, that they shall say, This [is] his wife: and they will kill me, but they will save thee alive. [Gen 12:12 KJV]Say, I pray thee, thou [art] my sister: that it may be well with me for thy sake; and my soul shall live because of thee. [Gen 12:13 KJV] And it came to pass, that, when Abram was come into Egypt, the Egyptians beheld the woman that she [was] very fair. [Gen 12:14 KJV] The princes also of Pharaoh saw her, and commended her before Pharaoh: and the woman was taken into Pharaoh's house. [Gen 12:15 KJV] And he entreated Abram well for her sake: and he had sheep, and oxen, and he asses, and menservants, and maidservants, and she asses, and camels. [Gen 12:16 KJV] And the LORD plagued Pharaoh and his house with great plagues because of Sarai Abram's wife. [Gen 12:17 KJV] And Pharaoh called Abram, and said, What [is] this [that] thou hast done unto me? why didst thou not tell me that she [was] thy wife? [Gen 12:18 KJV] Why saidst thou, She [is] my sister? so I might have taken her to me to wife: now therefore behold thy wife, take [her], and go thy way. [Gen 12:19 KJV]And Pharaoh commanded [his] men concerning him: and they sent him away, and his wife, and all that he had. [Gen 12:20 KJV]

CHAPTER 13

ABRAM SEPARATES FROM LOT

Abrams Wealth – Abram was very wealthy and his wealth continued to increase, this is an indication that God has no problem with His people having wealth; we do not have to wait to get to the book of Joshua to find an example of God giving us power to get wealth.

And Abram [was] very rich in cattle, in silver, and in gold. [Gen 13:2 KJV]

Abram at Bethel – this was the second time that Abram journeyed to Bethel and again he called on the name of Jehovah.

And he went on his journeys from the south even to Bethel, unto the place where his tent had been at the beginning, between Bethel and Hai; [Gen 13:3 KJV] Unto the place of the altar, which he had made there at the first: and there Abram called on the name of the LORD. [Gen 13:4 KJV]

Lots Wealth – Lot was wealthy also, but he also enjoyed the benefit of being covered by Abram as his father naturally and spiritually, he was enjoying the blessing of Abram, remember, Lot was choosing to stay with Abram, he was following him, he was not being forced to stay or to submit to Abram's authority, but notice what happens later on when he leaves his covering.

And Lot also, which went with Abram, had flocks, and herds, and tents. [Gen 13:5 KJV]

Family Strife – Abram has to now ask Lot to leave - Abram and Lot have so much wealth the land was not able to bear it. This led to strife among their headmen, now we have come to the time of separation. I can imagine that there was more than one incidence of strife because Abram had many opportunities to ask Lot to leave but he did not, he should have not brought Lot with him in the first place, but he must have felt some responsibility to take care of his brother's child after his brother died.

The father in Abram was working and he wanted to make sure that Lot had what he needed. This would not have been unusual for Abram since his father, Terah had all of his adult children with him and they all lived together until God told him to leave his kindred and his father's house. Sometimes in our family dynamics we find ourselves dealing with adult children the same way, they may not be able to leave home immediately, but they do mature to the point where they want to run the house as if it were theirs. That is natural because they must be able to manage their own home, but when it gets close to the time that they should leave strife sets into the family fellowship and they are usually forced to leave because their parents are not going to give them control of their home.

And the land was not able to bear them, that they might dwell together: for their substance was great, so that they could not dwell together. [Gen 13:6 KJV]And there was a strife between the herdmen of Abram's cattle and the herdmen of Lot's cattle: and the Canaanite and the Perizzite dwelled then in the land. [Gen 13:7 KJV] And Abram said unto Lot, Let there be no strife, I pray thee, between me and thee, and between my herdmen and thy herdmen; for we [be] brethren. [Gen 13:8 KJV] [Is] not the whole land before thee? separate thyself, I pray thee, from me: if [thou wilt take] the left hand, then I will go to the right; or if [thou depart] to the right hand, then I will go to the left. [Gen 13:9 KJV]

Separation Terms - Abram had provided an inheritance for Lot, he had wealth to take care of himself and his family and Abram knew that Lot would be able to survive without him but he still had a fathering attitude toward Lot. We know from Psalm 13 that a good man leaves an inheritance for his children's children. He had not positioned himself to lose his wealth to the just. Abram had no children at this time and it must have been an honor for him to have Lot as a son.

A good [man] leaveth an inheritance to his children's children: and the wealth of the sinner [is] laid up for the just. [Pro 13:22 KJV] And Lot lifted up his eyes, and beheld all the plain of Jordan, that it [was] well watered everywhere, before the LORD destroyed Sodom and Gomorrah, [even] as the garden of the LORD, like the land of Egypt, as thou comest unto Zoar. [Gen 13:10 KJV]

Leave Covering - Notice that Lot did not experience any trouble until he begin to desire separation from his father Abram, he never considered what his father needed, he focused on his need and agreed to leave and go to what seem to be a comfortable prosperous place. He remember the fertile land in Egypt and when he saw the land near Sodom seem to be like what he saw in Egypt he was more than happy to go there. This is a great lesson for believers, because we see the wealth of the wicked and then we try to get it the way they did instead of remembering that it is laid up for the just. Why join the wicked in their doings and expect to keep our wealth, it will eventually be taken and given to the just.

Then Lot chose him all the plain of Jordan; and Lot journeyed east: and they separated themselves the one from the other. [Gen 13:11 KJV] But the men of Sodom [were] wicked and sinners before the LORD exceedingly. [Gen 13:13 KJV] Abram dwelled in the land of Canaan, and Lot dwelled in the cities of the plain, and pitched [his] tent toward Sodom. [Gen 13:12 KJV]

God Speaks to Abram and promises inheritance of land and gives him instructions to walk through the land. Can you imagine what Abram must have been thinking since he had no children at that time? He did not even ask God how, when or where, he just believed him. This is the foundation of faith; we cannot consider the how, when or where we must believe we have what God said now. In addition God told Abram to walk through the land, in the length and breadth of it. This is the dynamic of this promise. **God gave to Abram something for billions of people that he would never see in his lifetime. That is the beginning of our understanding that what God gives to us is not small and it is not just for us and unless He returns before we leave the planet it cannot be done in our lifetime.**

And the LORD said unto Abram, after that Lot was separated from him, Lift up now thine eyes, and look from the place where thou art northward, and southward, and eastward, and westward: [Gen 13:14 KJV]For all the land which thou seest, to thee will I give it, and to thy seed for ever. [Gen 13:15 KJV] And I will make thy seed as the dust of the earth: so that if a man can number the dust of the earth, [then] shall thy seed also be numbered. [Gen 13:16 KJV]Arise, walk through the land in the length of it and in the breadth of it; for I will give it unto thee. [Gen 13:17 KJV] Then Abram removed [his] tent, and came and dwelt in the plain of Mamre, which [is] in Hebron, and built there an altar unto the LORD. [Gen 13:18 KJV]

CHAPTER 14

ABRAM GIVES TITHES AND OFFERINGS

The Capture of Lot – Lot found himself in the middle of a war against the kings of Sodom and Gomorrah and was captured and taken off as captive. Now the beauty of the land that he wanted had brought him to this point in his life.

And they took Lot, Abram's brother's son, who dwelt in Sodom, and his goods, and departed. [Gen 14:12 KJV]

[That these] made war with Bera king of Sodom, and with Birsha king of Gomorrah, Shinab king of Admah, and Shemeber king of Zeboiim, and the king of Bela, which is Zoar. [Gen 14:2 KJV] All these were joined together in the vale of Siddim, which is the salt sea. [Gen 14:3 KJV] Twelve years they served Chedorlaomer, and in the thirteenth year they rebelled. [Gen 14:4 KJV]And there went out the king of Sodom, and the king of Gomorrah, and the king of Admah, and the king of Zeboiim, and the king of Bela (the same [is] Zoar;) and they joined battle with them in the vale of Siddim; [Gen 14:8 KJV]With Chedorlaomer the king of Elam, and with Tidal king of nations, and Amraphel king of Shinar, and Arioch king of Ellasar; four kings with five. [Gen 14:9 KJV] And they took all the goods of Sodom and Gomorrah, and all their victuals, and went their way. [Gen 14:11 KJV]

Abram hears about what had happened to Lot and immediately made plans to rescue him. **He spoke of him as his brother and at that point became his brother's keeper.** This is exciting to me because Abram with the help of God was able to defeat the warriors of all of these kings with his small band of people. He had only **three hundred and eighteen people fighting with him.**

And there came one that had escaped, and told Abram the Hebrew; for he dwelt in the plain of Mamre the Amorite, brother of Eshcol, and brother of Aner: and these [were] confederate with Abram. [Gen 14:13 KJV] And when Abram heard that his brother was taken captive, he armed his trained [servants], born in his own house, three hundred and eighteen, and pursued [them] unto Dan. [Gen 14:14 KJV] And he divided himself against them, he and his servants, by night, and smote them, and pursued them unto Hobah, which [is] on the left hand of Damascus. [Gen 14:15 KJV]And he brought back all the goods, and also brought again his brother Lot, and his goods, and the women also, and the people. [Gen 14:16 KJV]

Abram meets Melchizedek – Abram receives bread and wine, communion, a covenant meal from the priest of the Most High God and gives him a tithe of all, this should settle the question of whether to give a tithe of the net or the gross of our income. Notice that Melchizedek did not ask for a tithe or an offering, it was given freely by Abram.

And Melchizedek king of Salem brought forth bread and wine: and he [was] the priest of the most high God. [Gen 14:18 KJV]And he blessed him, and said, Blessed [be] Abram of the most high God, possessor of heaven and earth: [Gen 14:19 KJV]And blessed be the most high God, which hath delivered thine enemies into thy hand. And he gave him tithes of all. [Gen 14:20 KJV]

Abram rejects anything from evil people – When the king of Sodom offered Abram the opportunity to keep the goods that he had brought back from the fight of rescuing Lot. Abram turned him down. Abram has settled in his heart that the LORD is his supply; he will give all of the credit of his wealth to the LORD only. He expected the LORD to help him rescue Lot and the LORD did. He did not try to force Lot to do what he did but he did live his life before Lot as a good example of how to live.

And the king of Sodom said unto Abram, Give me the persons, and take the goods to thyself. [Gen 14:21 KJV] And Abram said to the king of Sodom, I have lift up mine hand unto the LORD, the most high God, the possessor of heaven and earth, [Gen 14:22 KJV]That I will not [take] from a thread even to a shoelatchet, and that I will not take any thing that [is] thine, lest thou shouldest say, I have made Abram rich: [Gen 14:23 KJV]Save only that which the young men have eaten, and the portion of the men which went with me, Aner, Eshcol, and Mamre; let them take their portion. [Gen 14:24 KJV]

CHAPTER 15

ABRAM COVENANTS WITH GOD

After the departure of Lot and while Abram was still living in the land that God had promised him God spoke to him again and now Abram begins to ask God questions, Abram had never questioned God before but now he is asking to get some answers. He now wants to know how God is going to give him what He has promised since he is childless. Abram wanted to know if God was going to use his servant Eliezer to bring all of this to pass since he had no child. God spoke to him and told him no, not Eliezer but your seed will come out of your bowels and Abram believed God and God counted that as righteousness.

After these things the word of the LORD came unto Abram in a vision, saying, Fear not, Abram: I [am] thy shield, [and] thy exceeding great reward. [Gen 15:1 KJV]And Abram said, Lord GOD, what wilt thou give me, seeing I go childless, and the steward of my house [is] this Eliezer of Damascus? [Gen 15:2 KJV] And Abram said, Behold, to me thou hast given no seed: and, lo, one born in my house is mine heir. [Gen 15:3 KJV]And, behold, the word of the LORD [came] unto him, saying, This shall not be thine heir; but he that shall come forth out of thine own bowels shall be thine heir. [Gen 15:4 KJV]And he brought him forth abroad, and said, Look now toward heaven, and tell the stars, if thou be able to number them: and he said unto him, So shall thy seed be. [Gen 15:5 KJV] And he believed in the LORD; and he counted it to him for righteousness. [Gen 15:6 KJV]

Abram believed God and now he wants to know, how he will know that he has all of this and God cut a covenant with him and told him how to prepare the offering for the covenant. Abram prepared the animal sacrifices as God had instructed him and he watched over them until the sun was going down. Then God put him in a deep sleep and begin to give him more information about the promises that were being made to him. God passed through the blood of the animals with fire and said to him:

❖ <u>**I brought you out to give you this land**</u> - *And he said unto him, I [am] the LORD that brought thee out of Ur of the Chaldees, to give thee this land to inherit it. [Gen 15:7 KJV]*

❖ <u>**God made a covenant with Abram**</u> - *And he said, Lord GOD, whereby shall I know that I shall inherit it? [Gen 15:8 KJV]And he said unto him, Take me an heifer of three years old, and a she goat of three years old, and a ram of three years old, and a turtledove, and a young pigeon. [Gen 15:9 KJV]And he took unto him all these, and divided them in the midst, and laid each piece one against another: but the birds divided he not. [Gen 15:10 KJV]And when the sun was going down, a deep sleep fell upon Abram; and, lo, an horror of great darkness fell upon him. [Gen 15:12 KJV]And he said unto Abram,*

❖ <u>**Your seed shall be a stranger in a land that is not theirs and shall be afflicted four hundred years**</u> - *Know of a surety that thy seed shall be a stranger in a land [that is] not theirs, and shall serve them; and they shall afflict them four hundred years; [Gen 15:13 KJV]*

❖ <u>**I will judge the nation that they serve and afterwards they shall come out with great substance**</u> - *And also that nation, whom they shall serve, will I judge: and afterward shall they come out with great substance. [Gen 15:14 KJV]*

❖ You shall go to your fathers in peace - *And thou shalt go to thy fathers in peace; thou shalt be buried in a good old age. [Gen 15:15 KJV]*

❖ But in the fourth generation they shall come hither again: for the iniquity of the Amorites [is] not yet full. [Gen 15:16 KJV]

At the same time God gave Abram details about the land and its inhabitants that were going to have to leave, after the fourth generation they would have to go. God gave them time for their iniquity to finish it course. These people are the people that are symbolic of the kingdoms of this world that Satan rules and Abrams seed was going to tear their kingdom down and the kingdoms of this world would become the kingdoms of our Lord and of His Christ and He shall reign forever.

And it came to pass, that, when the sun went down, and it was dark, behold a smoking furnace, and a burning lamp that passed between those pieces. [Gen 15:17 KJV]In the same day the LORD made a covenant with Abram, saying, Unto thy seed have I given this land, from the river of Egypt unto the great river, the river Euphrates: [Gen 15:18 KJV] The Kenites, and the Kenizzites, and the Kadmonites, [Gen 15:19 KJV] And the Hittites, and the Perizzites, and the Rephaims, [Gen 15:20 KJV] And the Amorites, and the Canaanites, and the Girgashites, and the Jebusites. [Gen 15:21 KJV]

CHAPTER 16

ABRAM'S SON OF THE FLESH

Sarai Abram's wife did not believe that she would be the one that God used to bring forth the promised child so she talks Abram into having a child with her maid Hagar, she bore him a son but this was not the child that the LORD had promised Abram and he became his son born of his will and his flesh. The name of this son was Ishmael.

Now Sarai Abram's wife bare him no children: and she had an handmaid, an Egyptian, whose name [was] Hagar. [Gen 16:1 KJV]And Sarai said unto Abram, Behold now, the LORD hath restrained me from bearing: I pray thee, go in unto my maid; it may be that I may obtain children by her. And Abram hearkened to the voice of Sarai. [Gen 16:2 KJV]And Hagar bare Abram a son: and Abram called his son's name, which Hagar bare, Ishmael. [Gen 16:15 KJV]And Abram [was] fourscore and six years old, when Hagar bare Ishmael to Abram. [Gen 16:16 KJV]

Note:

Study topic for students - Hagar was the first single mother:

- What lessons can be learned from her experience?

_____

_____

_____

_____

_____

- Compare those lessons with what happens to single mothers and fathers today?

_____

_____

_____

CHAPTER 17

ABRAM AND SARAI GET A NAME CHANGE FROM GOD

Abram = 'exalted father' is given a new name by God Abraham = 'father of a multitude' or "chief of multitude" Then God explained the details of this covenant with Him, Abraham and Abraham's seed. God commands him to circumcise all males even the servants as a token of this covenant.

And when Abram was ninety years old and nine, the LORD appeared to Abram, and said unto him, I [am] the Almighty God; walk before me, and be thou perfect. [Gen 17:1 KJV]And I will make my covenant between me and thee, and will multiply thee exceedingly. [Gen 17:2 KJV]As for me, behold, my covenant [is] with thee, and thou shalt be a father of many nations. [Gen 17:4 KJV]Neither shall thy name any more be called Abram, but thy name shall be Abraham; for a father of many nations have I made thee. [Gen 17:5 KJV]And I will make thee exceeding fruitful, and I will make nations of thee, and kings shall come out of thee. [Gen 17:6 KJV]This [is] my covenant, which ye shall keep, between me and you and thy seed after thee; Every man child among you shall be circumcised. [Gen 17:10 KJV]And ye shall circumcise the flesh of your foreskin; and it shall be a token of the covenant betwixt me and you. [Gen 17:11 KJV]And he that is eight days old shall be circumcised among you, every man child in your generations, he that is born in the house, or bought with money of any stranger, which [is] not of thy seed. [Gen 17:12 KJV]And the uncircumcised man child whose flesh of his foreskin is not circumcised, that soul shall be cut off from his people; he hath broken my covenant. [Gen 17:14 KJV]

Then God told Abraham of the name change of his wife Sarai = 'princess' to Sarah = 'noblewoman' and she would bear him a son and that he was to call his name Isaac and God said to Abraham - I will bless her, and she shall be [a mother] of nations; kings of people shall be of her. Now Abraham realizes that he will be having another son at age one hundred and he is over joyed with his exceeding great reward from God.

And God said unto Abraham, As for Sarai thy wife, thou shalt not call her name Sarai, but Sarah [shall] her name [be]. [Gen 17:15 KJV] And I will bless her, and give thee a son also of her: yea, I will bless her, and she shall be [a mother] of nations; kings of people shall be of her. [Gen 17:16 KJV]Then

Abraham fell upon his face, and laughed, and said in his heart, Shall [a child] be born unto him that is an hundred years old? and shall Sarah, that is ninety years old, bear? [Gen 17:17 KJV]

After God told Abraham that Sarah his wife would bear him a son he inquired about Ishmael. God answered giving him the understanding that the covenant was with Isaac and his seed but He had already blessed Ismael and then God told Abraham how he had blessed Ismael. Abraham was ninety nine years old and Ishmael was thirteen years old when they were circumcised.

And God said, Sarah thy wife shall bear thee a son indeed; and thou shalt call his name Isaac: and I will establish my covenant with him for an everlasting covenant, [and] with his seed after him. [Gen 17:19 KJV]And as for Ishmael, I have heard thee: Behold, I have blessed him, and will make him fruitful, and will multiply him exceedingly; twelve princes shall he beget, and I will make him a great nation. [Gen 17:20 KJV]But my covenant will I establish with Isaac, which Sarah shall bear unto thee at this set time in the next year. [Gen 17:21 KJV]And Abraham [was] ninety years old and nine, when he was circumcised in the flesh of his foreskin. [Gen 17:24 KJV]And Ishmael his son [was] thirteen years old, when he was circumcised in the flesh of his foreskin. [Gen 17:25 KJV]

CHAPTER 18

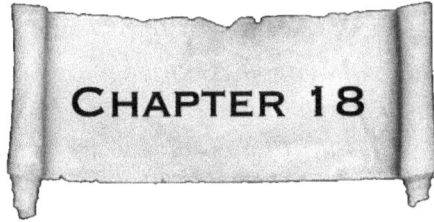

ABRAHAM PLEADS FOR SODOM AND GOMORRAH

The LORD appeared to Abraham in the plains and Abraham invited Him into his home, he prepared a meal for them and they agreed to visit with him, during that time the Lord told him of the time of the birth of his son Isaac and Sarah did overhear the conversation. Now that the time is close God allowed Sarah to hear for herself that she was about to have a child, she had some challenges believing and she laughed within herself. Now this is interesting, God did not ask Sarah why she laughed, He asked Abraham and then God asked him is anything too hard for God? Abraham was her covering and he should have been able to raise her faith up a level, she denied laughing because she was afraid, but the LORD confirmed His promise to Abraham and Sarah and started to leave.

And the LORD appeared unto him in the plains of Mamre: and he sat in the tent door in the heat of the day; [Gen 18:1 KJV] And he lift up his eyes and looked, and, lo, three men stood by him: and when he saw [them], he ran to meet them from the tent door, and bowed himself toward the ground, [Gen 18:2 KJV]And Abraham hastened into the tent unto Sarah, and said, Make ready quickly three measures of fine meal, knead [it], and make cakes upon the hearth. [Gen 18:6 KJV]And they said unto him, Where [is] Sarah thy wife? And he said, Behold, in the tent. [Gen 18:9 KJV] And he said, I will certainly return unto thee according to the time of life; and, lo, Sarah thy wife shall have a son. And Sarah heard [it] in the tent door, which [was] behind him. [Gen 18:10 KJV] Now Abraham and Sarah [were] old [and] well stricken in age; [and] it ceased to be with Sarah after the manner of women. [Gen 18:11 KJV]Therefore Sarah laughed within herself, saying, After I am waxed old shall I have pleasure, my lord being old also? [Gen 18:12 KJV]And the LORD said unto Abraham, Wherefore did Sarah laugh, saying, Shall I of a surety bear a child, which am old? [Gen 18:13 KJV] Is any thing too hard for the LORD? At the time appointed I will return unto thee, according to the time of life, and Sarah shall have a son. [Gen 18:14 KJV]Then Sarah denied, saying, I laughed not; for she was afraid. And he said, Nay; but thou didst laugh. [Gen 18:15 KJV]

The LORD shared with Abraham what He planned to do at Sodom:

And the LORD said, Because the cry of Sodom and Gomorrah is great, and because their sin is very grievous; [Gen 18:20 KJV]I will go down now, and see whether they have done altogether according to the cry of it, which is come unto me; and if not, I will know. [Gen 18:21 KJV]And the men turned their faces from thence, and went toward Sodom: but Abraham stood yet before the LORD. [Gen 18:22 KJV]

Abraham begins to plead for the city, he knew that Lot was there and he ask the LORD to save the city if He could find a certain number of righteous there. Abraham asked for fifty and the LORD said yes, then he asked for forty five and the LORD said yes, then he asked for Forty and the LORD said yes and finally he ask to save the city for ten and the LORD said I will not destroy for the sake of ten.

And Abraham drew near, and said, Wilt thou also destroy the righteous with the wicked? [Gen 18:23 KJV] Peradventure there be fifty righteous within the city: wilt thou also destroy and not spare the place for the fifty righteous that [are] therein? [Gen 18:24 KJV]And the LORD said, If I find in Sodom fifty righteous within the city, then I will spare all the place for their sakes. [Gen 18:26 KJV] Peradventure there shall lack five of the fifty righteous: wilt thou destroy all the city for [lack of] five? And he said, If I find there forty and five, I will not destroy [it]. [Gen 18:28 KJV]And he said [unto him], Oh let not the Lord be angry, and I will speak: Peradventure there shall thirty be found there. And he said, I will not do [it], if I find thirty there. [Gen 18:30 KJV]And he said, Behold now, I have taken upon me to speak unto the Lord: Peradventure there shall be twenty found there. And he said, I will not destroy [it] for twenty's sake. [Gen 18:31 KJV] And he said, Oh let not the Lord be angry, and I will speak yet but this once: Peradventure ten shall be found there. And he said, I will not destroy [it] for ten's sake. [Gen 18:32 KJV]

CHAPTER 19

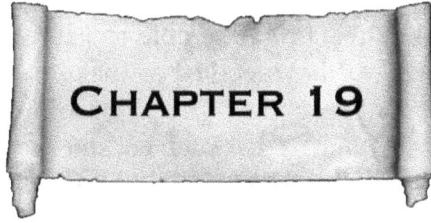

SODOM AND GOMORRAH DESTROYED

LOT AND HIS DAUGHTERS SAVED

Remember when the LORD appeared to Abraham there were three of them but only two of them went on to Sodom and Gomorrah. They did not even want to stay in Lot's house but he begged them to stay and when they entered the house some men of the city wanted to force them into a same sex sexual relationship. They blinded the men and they scattered but they concluded that the report that had come up to heaven about the condition of the city was true and proceeded to remove Lot and his family before they destroyed the cities. Lot wanted to take the husbands of his daughters but they thought it was a joke and did not follow him out of the city. That must have been difficult for Lot because he did not have enough influence to convince them to leave. Lot's wife went with him but she looked back and became a pillar of salt.

And there came two angels to Sodom at even; and Lot sat in the gate of Sodom: and Lot seeing [them] rose up to meet them; and he bowed himself with his face toward the ground; [Gen 19:1 KJV] Behold now, I have two daughters which have not known man; let me, I pray you, bring them out unto you, and do ye to them as [is] good in your eyes: only unto these men do nothing; for therefore came they under the shadow of my roof. [Gen 19:8 KJV]But the men put forth their hand, and pulled Lot into the house to them, and shut to the door. [Gen 19:10 KJV]For we will destroy this place, because the cry of them is waxen great before the face of the LORD; and the LORD hath sent us to destroy it. [Gen 19:13 KJV]And Lot went out, and spake unto his sons in law, which married his daughters, and said, Up, get you out of this place; for the LORD will destroy this city. But he seemed as one that mocked unto his sons in law. [Gen 19:14 KJV] And when the morning arose, then the angels hastened Lot, saying, Arise, take thy wife, and thy two daughters, which are here; lest thou be consumed in the iniquity of the city. [Gen 19:15 KJV]Then the LORD rained upon Sodom and upon Gomorrah brimstone and fire from the LORD out of heaven; [Gen 19:24 KJV]And he overthrew those cities, and all the plain, and all the inhabitants of the cities, and that which grew upon the ground. [Gen 19:25 KJV]

Lot and his daughters feared the city so they decided to live in a cave. His two daughters decided that they would not be able to get a man and no man on the earth would come to them so they decided to make their father drunk and get him to give each one of them a child. They took turns over a two day period each went in and lay with their father and became pregnant with a son. The name of the first born daughter's son was Moab, who is the father of the Moabites unto this day (Ruth was a decedent of his). The name of the son of the younger daughter was Benammi: who is the father of the children of Ammon unto this day.

Abraham loved Lot and this did not go unnoticed by the LORD, because He included Lot's family in the bloodline of Jesus Christ. As we continue our study of the Old Testament you will see these people appear and now you can remember from where they came. It is not surprising that Lot's daughters come up with this idea of incest as a good solution to a temporary problem since they had both spent so much time in Sodom. They were convinced that they would never have an opportunity to get a husband and they settled for incest.

And Lot went up out of Zoar, and dwelt in the mountain, and his two daughters with him; for he feared to dwell in Zoar: and he dwelt in a cave, he and his two daughters. [Gen 19:30 KJV] And the firstborn said unto the younger, Our father [is] old, and [there is] not a man in the earth to come in unto us after the manner of all the earth: [Gen 19:31 KJV]Come, let us make our father drink wine, and we will lie with him, that we may preserve seed of our father. [Gen 19:32 KJV] And they made their father drink wine that night: and the firstborn went in, and lay with her father; and he perceived not when she lay down, nor when she arose. [Gen 19:33 KJV]And it came to pass on the morrow, that the firstborn said unto the younger, Behold, I lay yesternight with my father: let us make him drink wine this night also; and go thou in, [and] lie with him, that we may preserve seed of our father. [Gen 19:34 KJV]And they made their father drink wine that night also: and the younger arose, and lay with him; and he perceived not when she lay down, nor when she arose. [Gen 19:35 KJV]Thus were both the daughters of Lot with child by their father. [Gen 19:36 KJV]And the firstborn bare a son, and called his name Moab: the same [is] the father of the Moabites unto this day. [Gen 19:37 KJV]And the younger, she also bare a son, and called his name Benammi: the same [is] the father of the children of Ammon unto this day. [Gen 19:38 KJV]

CHAPTER 20

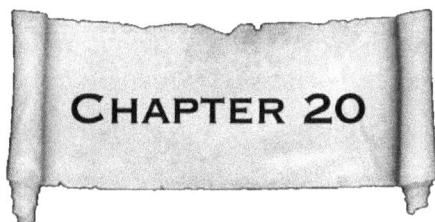

ABRAHAM'S ENCOUNTER WITH KING ABIMELECH OF GERAR

God had given Abraham directions to walk the land, all of the land that He had given him and his seed via Isaac. Abraham was obedient and did as The LORD had commanded him; however he still feared that his life was in danger because of the beauty of his wife Sarah. Once again he asked her to pretend that she was his sister and she agreed. God had promised Abraham that whoever blessed him He would bless and whoever cursed him He would curse. Abraham did not rely on this promise when it came to this particular situation perhaps because he knew that was a common practice at that time, however God kept His promise, and protected Sarah from the harm of being used against her will.

And Abraham journeyed from thence toward the south country, and dwelled between Kadesh and Shur, and sojourned in Gerar. [Gen 20:1 KJV] And Abraham said of Sarah his wife, She [is] my sister: and Abimelech king of Gerar sent, and took Sarah. [Gen 20:2 KJV]

But God came to Abimelech in a dream by night, and said to him, Behold, thou [art but] a dead man, for the woman which thou hast taken; for she [is] a man's wife. [Gen 20:3 KJV] Of course Abimelech said that he did not know she was Abraham's wife and God responded with instructions to Abimelech as how to handle Sarah. *And God said unto him in a dream, Yea, I know that thou didst this in the integrity of thy heart; for I also withheld thee from sinning against me: therefore suffered I thee not to touch her. [Gen 20:6 KJV]*

Abimelech informed his servants and they were all afraid, they had done nothing but were all affected by what their king had done. The authority of one man had affected the entire nation **(one man caused everyone to have to struggle with sin and death and one man caused whosoever that would believe on Him to be redeemed from sin and death).** *Therefore Abimelech rose early in the morning, and called all his servants, and told all these things in their ears: and the men were sore afraid. [Gen 20:8 KJV]*

Abimelech ask Abraham why Sarah was said to be his sister and he told him about the plan that the two of them came up with to save his life during the process of their travel.

And it came to pass, when God caused me to wander from my father's house, that I said unto her, This [is] thy kindness which thou shalt shew unto me; at every place whither we shall come, say of me, He [is] my brother. [Gen 20:13 KJV]

Abimelech returned Sarah to Abraham and gave him offerings. Now it is up to Abraham to remove the curse that God had put on Abimelech. This is very interesting because we never consider giving gifts to someone that may have caused us harm, but that is exactly what Abimelech did. God had closed the womb of Abimelech's entire house and it was Abraham that reversed that curse. This is an example of how Jesus told us that we should treat our enemies. This is the Old Testament, but Abraham followed the principle that Jesus taught in Matthew chapter 5:

But I say unto you, Love your enemies, bless them that curse you, do good to them that hate you, and pray for them which despitefully use you, and persecute you; [Mat 5:44 KJV]

Some of us may love our enemies and some of us may pray for them but not many of us would give them a gift (do good to them) as what happened in the this passage:

And Abimelech took sheep, and oxen, and menservants, and womenservants, and gave [them] unto Abraham, and restored him Sarah his wife. [Gen 20:14 KJV]And unto Sarah he said, Behold, I have given thy brother a thousand [pieces] of silver: behold, he [is] to thee a covering of the eyes, unto all that [are] with thee, and with all [other]: thus she was reproved. [Gen 20:16 KJV] So Abraham prayed unto God: and God healed Abimelech, and his wife, and his maidservants; and they bare [children]. [Gen 20:17 KJV] For the LORD had fast closed up all the wombs of the house of Abimelech, because of Sarah Abraham's wife. [Gen 20:18 KJV]

CHAPTER 21

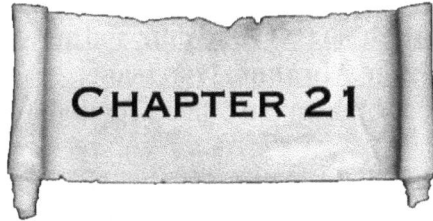

THE BIRTH OF ISAAC

The LORD visited Sarah and she conceived and when their son was born Abraham named him Isaac as the LORD had commanded him. Ishmael is now a teenager and he begins mocking Isaac. This should have been expected by his mother Hagar because of the word that was spoken over him before he was born.

And he will be a wild man; his hand [will be] against every man, and every man's hand against him; and he shall dwell in the presence of all his brethren. [Gen 16:12 KJV]

When Sarah saw the mocking of her son, she asked Abraham to send them away because Hagar's son would not share in the inheritance with her son, this grieved Abraham, but God spoke to Abraham and asked him not to grieve and told him that he would make a great nation out of Ishmael and then told him to obey his wife Sarah and send them away.

And the LORD visited Sarah as he had said, and the LORD did unto Sarah as he had spoken. [Gen 21:1 KJV]For Sarah conceived, and bare Abraham a son in his old age, at the set time of which God had spoken to him. [Gen 21:2 KJV] And Abraham called the name of his son that was born unto him, whom Sarah bare to him, Isaac. [Gen 21:3 KJV]And Abraham was an hundred years old, when his son Isaac was born unto him. [Gen 21:5 KJV]And the child grew, and was weaned: and Abraham made a great feast the [same] day that Isaac was weaned. [Gen 21:8 KJV]And Sarah saw the son of Hagar the Egyptian, which she had born unto Abraham, mocking. [Gen 21:9 KJV]Wherefore she said unto Abraham, Cast out this bondwoman and her son: for the son of this bondwoman shall not be heir with my son, [even] with Isaac. [Gen 21:10 KJV]And the thing was very grievous in Abraham's sight because of his son. [Gen 21:11 KJV]And God said unto Abraham, Let it not be grievous in thy sight because of the lad, and because of thy bondwoman; in all that Sarah hath said unto thee, hearken unto her voice; for in Isaac shall thy seed be called. [Gen 21:12 KJV]And also of the son of the bondwoman will I make a nation, because he [is] thy seed. [Gen 21:13 KJV]

It is now time for the bonds woman and her son to leave. God had promised the inheritance to the son of the married woman not the bondwoman. **Sarah was on**

point because we as believes are the sons of God and our husband is the one that was the only begotten son of God our Father. We are the ones that have the inheritance from Abraham via Isaac. We have no inheritance from God via Ishmael. Abraham gave them food and water and sent them on their way.

The bondwoman and her son left but ran out of water in the process of transition. Hagar thought that Ishmael was going to die so she placed him out of her sight so that she would not have to watch him die, however she did not remember the word God had given her about her son's adult life, if she had understood she would have known that he could not die until he had accomplished the word that the LORD had spoken over his life. God heard the voice of her son and showed her where the water was then assured her that He would make him a great nation.

And Abraham rose up early in the morning, and took bread, and a bottle of water, and gave [it] unto Hagar, putting [it] on her shoulder, and the child, and sent her away: and she departed, and wandered in the wilderness of Beersheba. [Gen 21:14 KJV]And the water was spent in the bottle, and she cast the child under one of the shrubs. [Gen 21:15 KJV]And she went, and sat her down over against [him] a good way off, as it were a bowshot: for she said, Let me not see the death of the child. And she sat over against [him], and lift up her voice, and wept. [Gen 21:16 KJV]And God heard the voice of the lad; and the angel of God called to Hagar out of heaven, and said unto her, What aileth thee, Hagar? fear not; for God hath heard the voice of the lad where he [is]. [Gen 21:17 KJV]Arise, lift up the lad, and hold him in thine hand; for I will make him a great nation. [Gen 21:18 KJV]

Abimelech notices how God was blessing Abraham and wanted to make sure that Abraham remembered his kindness toward him, and asked him to swear that he would not deal falsely with him. Abraham did swear but he told Abimelech of how his servants had taken the well that he dug violently from him and Abimelech said that he was not told of this. Then Abraham gave Abimelech sheep and oxen and set seven ewe lambs as to let him know that he indeed had dug the well. The two men made a covenant that day and Abraham lived in the land of the Philistine's for some time after that meeting.

And it came to pass at that time, that Abimelech and Phichol the chief captain of his host spake unto Abraham, saying, God [is] with thee in all that thou doest: [Gen 21:22 KJV]Now therefore swear unto me here by God that thou wilt not deal falsely with me, nor with my son, nor with my son's son: [but] according to the kindness that I have done unto thee, thou shalt do unto me, and to the land wherein thou hast sojourned. [Gen 21:23 KJV]

CHAPTER 22

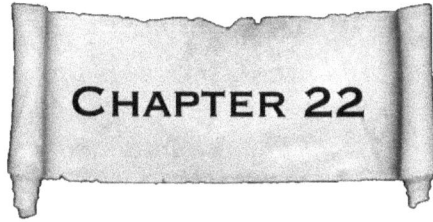

GOD ASK ABRAHAM FOR ISAAC

After all of these things happened God spoke to Abraham and told him to take Isaac to the mountain that he would tell him of and offer Isaac as a burnt offering Abraham did not question God; he rose up early the next morning and started out to do what God had commanded him to do. Now Isaac is Abraham's only begotten son he has waited for one hundred years to have this son and now God is asking him to give him up as a sacrifice. This indicates a level of growth with Abraham because he remembers that God said that He was giving Abraham an inheritance that will also be for his seed. Now he understands that Isaac is the seed that God had given him and whatever God is asking of him, he is in agreement with God. He understands that God is going to fulfill the words that were spoken over his life.

And it came to pass after these things, that God did tempt Abraham, and said unto him, Abraham: and he said, Behold, [here] I [am]. [Gen 22:1 KJV]And he said, Take now thy son, thine only [son] Isaac, whom thou lovest, and get thee into the land of Moriah; and offer him there for a burnt offering upon one of the mountains which I will tell thee of. [Gen 22:2 KJV]And Abraham rose up early in the morning, and saddled his ass, and took two of his young men with him, and Isaac his son, and clave the wood for the burnt offering, and rose up, and went unto the place of which God had told him. [Gen 22:3 KJV]

Now what happen next is interesting, because **on the 3rd day Abraham looked up and saw the place where his only begotten son was to give his life! This is a fore shadow of what happened to Jesus, now we have a person in the earth that is about to do in the earth with his son what God our Father has planned to do with His only Begotten Son.** And what is even more interesting is what Abraham said to his savants, you men stay here with the ass and I and the lad will go up and worship and come again to you. Abraham knew that he was going to sacrifice Isaac yet he told the young men that they both were coming back after they worshiped. Abraham must have expected God to raise Isaac from the dead. Isaac did ask his father where is the lamb that we are going to use and Abraham said that God would provide himself a lamb for a burnt offering. And we know that is exactly what God did provided himself a lamb who was His only begotten son in the person Jesus Christ who is also the Lamb of God.

Then on the third day Abraham lifted up his eyes, and saw the place afar off. [Gen 22:4 KJV] And Abraham said unto his young men, Abide ye here with the ass; and I and the lad will go yonder and worship, and come again to you. [Gen 22:5 KJV] And Abraham took the wood of the burnt offering, and laid [it] upon Isaac his son; and he took the fire in his hand, and a knife; and they went both of them together. [Gen 22:6 KJV] And Isaac spake unto Abraham his father, and said, My father: and he said, Here [am] I, my son. And he said, Behold the fire and the wood: but where [is] the lamb for a burnt offering? [Gen 22:7 KJV] And Abraham said, My son, God will provide himself a lamb for a burnt offering: so they went both of them together. [Gen 22:8 KJV]

Abraham built the altar, laid the wood upon it, bound his son Isaac and placed him upon the wood and stretched out his hand to slay his son and God called him and stopped him, told him not to harm the boy for now **I know that you fear Me seeing that you have not withheld your son, your only son from me. This is a first for Abraham and a first for God using Abraham this way. Can God ask you to do something that has never been done before and you trust Him even when it seems to be to your own hurt?** Isaac was not a small child; he helped his father carry the wood so he had to trust his father and corporate with being the sacrifice just as Abraham had to trust his father God.

And they came to the place which God had told him of; and Abraham built an altar there, and laid the wood in order, and bound Isaac his son, and laid him on the altar upon the wood. [Gen 22:9 KJV] And Abraham stretched forth his hand, and took the knife to slay his son. [Gen 22:10 KJV] And the angel of the LORD called unto him out of heaven, and said, Abraham, Abraham: and he said, Here [am] I. [Gen 22:11 KJV] And he said, Lay not thine hand upon the lad, neither do thou any thing unto him: for now I know that thou fearest God, seeing thou hast not withheld thy son, thine only [son] from me. [Gen 22:12 KJV]

Then Abraham saw the sacrifice, a ram caught in the thicket and he offered the ram instead of his son and God spoke to Abraham again and said because you have done this and did not withhold your son from me in blessing I will bless you, and in multiplying I will multiply your seed and as the stars of the heaven and the sand which is upon the sea shore your seed shall possess the gate of his enemies and all the nations of the earth shall be blessed because you have obeyed my voice. Abraham left that place and went to Beersheba and dwelt there.

And Abraham lifted up his eyes, and looked, and behold behind [him] a ram caught in a thicket by his horns: and Abraham went and took the ram, and offered him up for a burnt offering in the stead of his son. [Gen 22:13

KJV]And Abraham called the name of that place Jehovahjireh: as it is said [to] this day, In the mount of the LORD it shall be seen. [Gen 22:14 KJV]And the angel of the LORD called unto Abraham out of heaven the second time, [Gen 22:15 JV]And said, By myself have I sworn, saith the LORD, for because thou hast done this thing, and hast not withheld thy son, thine only [son]: [Gen 22:16 KJV]That in blessing I will bless thee, and in multiplying I will multiply thy seed as the stars of the heaven, and as the sand which [is] upon the sea shore; and thy seed shall possess the gate of his enemies; [Gen 22:17 KJV]And in thy seed shall all the nations of the earth be blessed; because thou hast obeyed my voice. [Gen 22:18 KJV]So Abraham returned unto his young men, and they rose up and went together to Beersheba; and Abraham dwelt at Beersheba. [Gen 22:19 KJV]

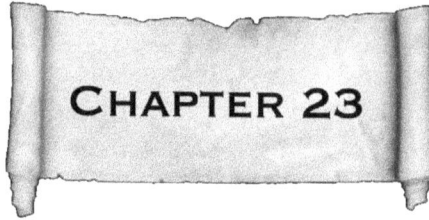

CHAPTER 23

ABRAHAM MOURNS THE DEATH OF SARAH

Sarah died at age one hundred and twenty seven in Hebron in the land of Canaan and Abraham purchased a burying place for her to be buried.

And Sarah was an hundred and seven and twenty years old: [these were] the years of the life of Sarah. [Gen 23:1 KJV]And Sarah died in Kirjatharba; the same [is] Hebron in the land of Canaan: and Abraham came to mourn for Sarah, and to weep for her. [Gen 23:2 KJV]And Abraham stood up from before his dead, and spake unto the sons of Heth, saying, [Gen 23:3 KJV]I [am] a stranger and a sojourner with you: give me a possession of a buryingplace with you, that I may bury my dead out of my sight. [Gen 23:4 KJV]My lord, hearken unto me: the land [is worth] four hundred shekels of silver; what [is] that betwixt me and thee? bury therefore thy dead. [Gen 23:15 KJV]And Abraham hearkened unto Ephron; and Abraham weighed to Ephron the silver, which he had named in the audience of the sons of Heth, four hundred shekels of silver, current [money] with the merchant. [Gen 23:16 KJV]And after this, Abraham buried Sarah his wife in the cave of the field of Machpelah before Mamre: the same [is] Hebron in the land of Canaan. [Gen 23:19 KJV]

Note:

Study questions for students:

- What was the significance of this burying place?

_____

_____

_____

- Who was later buried in this same place?

_____

_____

_____

_____

CHAPTER 24

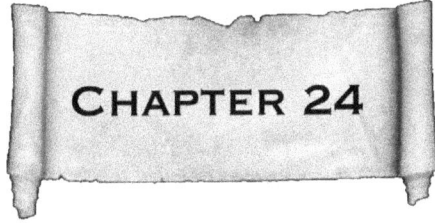

ABRAHAM SECURES A WIFE FOR ISAAC

In Abraham's old age being blessed of the LORD in all things Abraham sought a wife for Isaac. He sent his servant to his people to get a wife for his son; however he would not let Isaac leave the land that God had given them. Abraham had his servant to give him his oath that he would do this for him and the servant was not released from the oath unless the woman would not follow him. This was Abraham's oldest servant and he ruled over all that he had. The servant brought gifts, jewels of gold and jewels of silver and clothes to give to the woman and her family. The servant prayed to God for a sign to know the woman that would be the choice and his prayer was answered. The woman was name Rebekah and she agreed to go with the servant to be the wife of Isaac.

And Abraham was old, [and] well stricken in age: and the LORD had blessed Abraham in all things. [Gen 24:1 KJV]And Abraham said unto his eldest servant of his house, that ruled over all that he had, Put, I pray thee, thy hand under my thigh: [Gen 24:2 KJV]But thou shalt go unto my country, and to my kindred, and take a wife unto my son Isaac. [Gen 24:4 KJV]The LORD God of heaven, which took me from my father's house, and from the land of my kindred, and which spake unto me, and that sware unto me, saying, Unto thy seed will I give this land; he shall send his angel before thee, and thou shalt take a wife unto my son from thence. [Gen 24:7 KJV]And if the woman will not be willing to follow thee, then thou shalt be clear from this my oath: only bring not my son thither again. [Gen 24:8 KJV]And let it come to pass, that the damsel to whom I shall say, Let down thy pitcher, I pray thee, that I may drink; and she shall say, Drink, and I will give thy camels drink also: [let the same be] she [that] thou hast appointed for thy servant Isaac; and thereby shall I know that thou hast shewed kindness unto my master. [Gen 24:14 KJV]And it came to pass, before he had done speaking, that, behold, Rebekah came out, who was born to Bethuel, son of Milcah, the wife of Nahor, Abraham's brother, with her pitcher upon her shoulder. [Gen 24:15 KJV]And the damsel [was] very fair to look upon, a virgin, neither had any man known her: and she went down to the well, and filled her pitcher, and came up. [Gen 24:16 KJV]And the servant brought forth jewels of silver, and jewels of gold, and raiment, and gave [them] to Rebekah: he gave also to her brother and to her mother precious things. [Gen 24:53 KJV]

Rebekah's family sent her and her nurse to Isaac to be married. Isaac married her and brought her into his mother's tent and he was comforted after his mother's death.

And they sent away Rebekah their sister, and her nurse, and Abraham's servant, and his men. [Gen 24:59 KJV]And they blessed Rebekah, and said unto her, Thou [art] our sister, be thou [the mother] of thousands of millions, and let thy seed possess the gate of those which hate them. [Gen 24:60 KJV]And Isaac brought her into his mother Sarah's tent, and took Rebekah, and she became his wife; and he loved her: and Isaac was comforted after his mother's [death]. [Gen 24:67 KJV]

CHAPTER 25

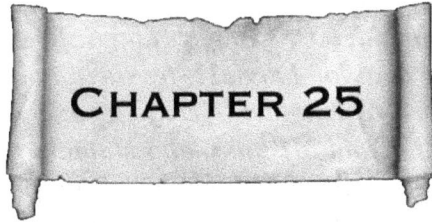

ABRAHAM MARRIES KETURAH AND MAKES HIS DEPARTURE

Abraham marries again to a woman by the name of Keturah and she bear him six sons and some of them had sons of their own all of which are listed in chapter 25, but Abraham while he was still living gave gifts to the sons of Keturah and sent them away from Isaac for he gave all he had to Isaac.

Abraham lived a hundred threescore and fifteen years, one hundred and seventy five years and died at a good old age which is one of the promises that the LORD had made to him, Isaac and Ishmael buried him with his wife Sarah.

Then again Abraham took a wife, and her name [was] Keturah. [Gen 25:1 KJV] And she bare him Zimran, and Jokshan, and Medan, and Midian, and Ishbak, and Shuah. [Gen 25:2 KJV]And Jokshan begat Sheba, and Dedan. And the sons of Dedan were Asshurim, and Letushim, and Leummim. [Gen 25:3 KJV]And the sons of Midian; Ephah, and Epher, and Hanoch, and Abida, and Eldaah. All these [were] the children of Keturah. [Gen 25:4 KJV]And Abraham gave all that he had unto Isaac. [Gen 25:5 KJV]But unto the sons of the concubines, which Abraham had, Abraham gave gifts, and sent them away from Isaac his son, while he yet lived, eastward, unto the east country. [Gen 25:6 KJV]And these [are] the days of the years of Abraham's life which he lived, an hundred threescore and fifteen years. [Gen 25:7 KJV]Then Abraham gave up the ghost, and died in a good old age, an old man, and full [of years]; and was gathered to his people. [Gen 25:8 KJV]The field which Abraham purchased of the sons of Heth: there was Abraham buried, and Sarah his wife. [Gen 25:10 KJV]

Near the end of chapter 25 the genealogy of the descendants of Ismael are listed and we see how God has kept His promise to Abraham and Hagar of the word He gave them concerning Ishmael. There were twelve princes, twelve nations born to him and they had towns and castles named after them. Notice that there were twelve of them and twelve is the number symbolic of divine government. Ishmael lived one hundred and thirty seven years and then he died.

Now these [are] the generations of Ishmael, Abraham's son, whom Hagar the Egyptian, Sarah's handmaid, bare unto Abraham: [Gen 25:12 KJV]And these [are] the names of the sons of Ishmael, by their names, according to their generations: the firstborn of Ishmael, Nebajoth; and Kedar, and Adbeel, and Mibsam, [Gen 25:13 KJV]And Mishma, and Dumah, and Massa, [Gen 25:14 KJV]Hadar, and Tema, Jetur, Naphish, and Kedemah: [Gen 25:15 KJV]These [are] the sons of Ishmael, and these [are] their names, by their towns, and by their castles; twelve princes according to their nations. [Gen 25:16 KJV]And these [are] the years of the life of Ishmael, an hundred and thirty and seven years: and he gave up the ghost and died; and was gathered unto his people. [Gen 25:17 KJV]And they dwelt from Havilah unto Shur, that [is] before Egypt, as thou goest toward Assyria: [and] he died in the presence of all his brethren. [Gen 25:18 KJV]

All of Abraham's children have been addressed and it is time to focus on the promise child Isaac. It is interesting to note that there are three different nations of people that call Abraham father and they all think that they are the chosen one by God; however the only one that is considered the promised child is Isaac. We will find even now in our time that people think because their father is Abraham that they have God on their side the same way that Isaac does. Keturah's children call Abraham their father and they say that they serve Jehovah, Ismael's children call Abraham father and they say that they serve Jehovah and all believe that they are accepted by God but only the ones who will accept the Lord Jesus Christ and believe on Him are accepted by God the Father Jehovah.

It does not matter whether they are descendants of Isaac, Ismael or Keturah they must all accept and believe by faith and confess with their mouth the Lord Jesus, and believe in their heart that God hath raised Jesus from the dead, they shalt be saved and be a part of the family of God. For some of them this is going to take a breaking away from tradition but this is a simple non complicated process for anybody on the planet.

The end of chapter 25 is the beginning of Isaac's story, he is forty years old when he married Rebekah and after a time he finds that she is barren, he prays to God about her condition and she becomes pregnant with twins that are fighting in the womb and she asked God about the trouble and God lets her know that she has two nations in her womb and the older will serve the younger. Isaac was sixty years old when they were born one was named Esau and his younger brother Jacob.

And these [are] the generations of Isaac, Abraham's son: Abraham begat Isaac: [Gen 25:19 KJV]And Isaac was forty years old when he took Rebekah to wife, the daughter of Bethuel the Syrian of Padanaram, the sister to Laban the Syrian. [Gen 25:20 KJV]And Isaac intreated the LORD for his wife, because she [was] barren: and the LORD was intreated of him, and Rebekah his wife conceived. [Gen 25:21 KJV]And the children struggled together within her; and she said, If [it be] so, why [am] I thus? And she went to enquire of the LORD. [Gen 25:22 KJV]And the LORD said unto her, Two nations [are] in thy womb, and two manner of people shall be separated from thy bowels; and [the one] people shall be stronger than [the other] people; and the elder shall serve the younger. [Gen 25:23 KJV]And when her days to be delivered were fulfilled, behold, [there were] twins in her womb. [Gen 25:24 KJV]And the first came out red, all over like an hairy garment; and they called his name Esau. [Gen 25:25 KJV]And after that came his brother out, and his hand took hold on Esau's heel; and his name was called Jacob: and Isaac [was] threescore years old when she bare them. [Gen 25:26 KJV]

As the boys grew Esau became a cunning hunter and his father Isaac loved him and their mother Rebekah loved Jacob. Notice that red seem to follow the life of Esau, he was covered with red hair when he was born and it was a red pottage that he sold his birthright to Jacob to be able to eat and from that his name was called Edom = 'red' , the color red is symbolic of suffering, sacrifice or sin. Esau despised his birthright.

And the boys grew: and Esau was a cunning hunter, a man of the field; and Jacob [was] a plain man, dwelling in tents. [Gen 25:27 KJV]And Isaac loved Esau, because he did eat of [his] venison: but Rebekah loved Jacob. [Gen 25:28 KJV]

We can see that the parents were not on one accord with their sons and this will play out later in a way that both do not expect. Esau was not interested in the inheritance that Isaac must have told them about. He was not interested in staying home to help take care of the sheep, he liked to hunt and be out in the field. This would be a problem if you are the one that must stay and take care of sheep if you do not desire to do so.

One day Esau came home from the field and wanted some food that Jacob had prepared, and Jacob refused to give it to him, unless he would give him his birthright. Esau thought so little of his birthright he sold it for one plate of food, he despised his birthright. He did not understand the importance of what that birthright meant. Later Esau would complain to Jacob about taking it from him but that did not happen, he sold it to Jacob, he obviously did not value his birthright because he said to Jacob I am at the point to die: and what profit shall this birthright do to me.

And Jacob sod pottage: and Esau came from the field, and he [was] faint: [Gen 25:29 KJV]And Esau said to Jacob, Feed me, I pray thee, with that same red [pottage]; for I [am] faint: therefore was his name called Edom. [Gen 25:30 KJV]And Jacob said, Sell me this day thy birthright. [Gen 25:31 KJV]And Esau said, Behold, I [am] at the point to die: and what profit shall this birthright do to me? [Gen 25:32 KJV]And Jacob said, Swear to me this day; and he sware unto him: and he sold his birthright unto Jacob. [Gen 25:33 KJV]Then Jacob gave Esau bread and pottage of lentiles; and he did eat and drink, and rose up, and went his way: thus Esau despised [his] birthright. [Gen 25:34 KJV]

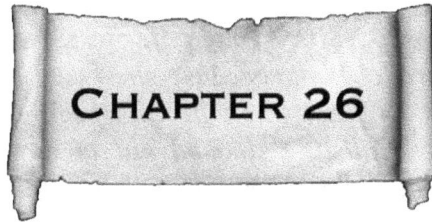

CHAPTER 26

ISAAC

Isaac and King Abimelech

Isaac is now faced with his first challenge of a famine in the land and hearing God for himself. The LORD appeared to him and told him not to go down to Egypt but to sojourn in this land which He was telling him of and he told Isaac and his seed and that He would be with him and bless him there, He would multiply his seed as the stars in the heaven and give him and them all these countries and He would perform the oath which he promised unto his father Abraham because Abraham obeyed His voice and kept his charge, His commandment, His statutes and His laws.

And there was a famine in the land, beside the first famine that was in the days of Abraham. And Isaac went unto Abimelech king of the Philistines unto Gerar. [Gen 26:1 KJV] And the LORD appeared unto him, and said, Go not down into Egypt; dwell in the land which I shall tell thee of: [Gen 26:2 KJV] Sojourn in this land, and I will be with thee, and will bless thee; for unto thee, and unto thy seed, I will give all these countries, and I will perform the oath which I sware unto Abraham thy father; [Gen 26:3 KJV] And I will make thy seed to multiply as the stars of heaven, and will give unto thy seed all these countries; and in thy seed shall all the nations of the earth be blessed; [Gen 26:4 KJV]Because that Abraham obeyed my voice, and kept my charge, my commandments, my statutes, and my laws. [Gen 26:5 KJV]And Isaac dwelt in Gerar: [Gen 26:6 KJV]

Isaac had a beautiful wife just as his mother had been and he did the same thing that his father did in regards to protecting himself from the men that may want to kill him to get his wife. Now he has to deal with Abimelech just as his father had done. Isaac told the men that asked about Rebekah that she was his sister, he was afraid that they would kill him for her. Abimelech saw them together and surmised that she was Isaac's wife and asked him why he had said she was his sister and he gave the same explanation that his father Abraham did for doing the same thing. Abimelech sent word that anyone who touches Isaac or his wife shall be put to death.

And the men of the place asked [him] of his wife; and he said, She [is] my sister: for he feared to say, [She is] my wife; lest, [said he], the men of the place should kill me for Rebekah; because she [was] fair to look upon. [Gen 26:7 KJV]And it came to pass, when he had been there a long time, that Abimelech king of the Philistines looked out at a window, and saw, and, behold, Isaac [was] sporting with Rebekah his wife. [Gen 26:8 KJV] And Abimelech called Isaac, and said, Behold, of a surety she [is] thy wife: and how saidst thou, She [is] my sister? And Isaac said unto him, Because I said, Lest I die for her. [Gen 26:9 KJV]And Abimelech said, What [is] this thou hast done unto us? one of the people might lightly have lien with thy wife, and thou shouldest have brought guiltiness upon us. [Gen 26:10 KJV]And Abimelech charged all [his] people, saying, He that toucheth this man or his wife shall surely be put to death. [Gen 26:11 KJV]

God had promised Isaac to bless him in the land where He had commanded him to stay rather than go down to Egypt. Isaac sowed in that land and received a hundred fold. Everything he had multiplied, his possessions became so great that the Philistines were jealous. Can you imagine the reward we would get if we were willing to submit ourselves as Isaac did? He was going to allow his father to kill him as a sacrifice to the LORD. When we know the word of God and do not submit to it we miss so many opportunities for multiplied blessings, when we do not submit to our fathers naturally and spiritually we miss so many opportunities for multiplied blessings. God gives us so many examples of how He loves his people and how He blesses them when they obey him. Remember what he told Isaac about his father Abraham **"And I will make thy seed to multiply as the stars of heaven, and will give unto thy seed all these countries; and in thy seed shall all the nations of the earth be blessed; [Gen 26:4 KJV]Because that Abraham obeyed my voice, and kept my charge, my commandments, my statutes, and my laws. [Gen 26:5 KJV]"** We must know how God deals with his people in their personal situations so we can know what to expect if we do the same.

The LORD multiplied Isaac so much that even king Abimelech was jealous; the people envied him and after Abraham died they filled all the wells that Abraham had dug with dirt. Isaac knew that he could not survive without water, his father had left wells that he could have used but the people would not let the wells stay open even to use them themselves. This could have been a hardship for Isaac, but he did not allow that to cause him to disobey God and leave the land to go where there was plenty of water, he dug more wells. Now if God were to give you this kind of wealth could you handle the pressure? Could you handle people that would hate you, envy you or be extremely jealous of you because of your prosperity? As we study the Old Testament we will see the LORD doing this for others as well, yet we need to be convinced and motivated in order to believe that He will do this for us.

Then Isaac sowed in that land, and received in the same year an hundredfold: and the LORD blessed him. [Gen 26:12 KJV] And the man waxed great, and went forward, and grew until he became very great: [Gen 26:13 KJV] For he had possession of flocks, and possession of herds, and great store of servants: and the Philistines envied him. [Gen 26:14 KJV] For all the wells which his father's servants had digged in the days of Abraham his father, the Philistines had stopped them, and filled them with earth.

Abimelech did not want Isaac to stay in the land, he had an issue with how the LORD was blessing Isaac, he began to see Isaac as a threat and forgot that it was the LORD doing this not Isaac, remember the promise to Abraham, I will bless those who bless you. He did not remember that blessing Isaac would cause him to be blessed also. He fell into the same trap that Eve did taking her eyes off of what she had to go after what she did not have as if that could ever be better. When God gives each one of us a word, nothing anybody else could offer could ever be better. What are you longing for that causes you to overlook what you already have?

Abimelech asked Isaac to leave because they were all afraid because he was greater than they were and therefore Isaac left and went to the valley of Gerar. Now he has trouble with the herdmen of Gerar, they contended with him about two of the wells and he had to abandon them

[Gen 26:15 KJV]And Abimelech said unto Isaac, Go from us; for thou art much mightier than we. [Gen 26:16 KJV] And Isaac departed thence, and pitched his tent in the valley of Gerar, and dwelt there. [Gen 26:17 KJV]And Isaac digged again the wells of water, which they had digged in the days of Abraham his father; for the Philistines had stopped them after the death of Abraham: and he called their names after the names by which his father had called them. [Gen 26:18 KJV]And Isaac's servants digged in the valley, and found there a well of springing water. [Gen 26:19 KJV]And the herdmen of Gerar did strive with Isaac's herdmen, saying, The water [is] ours: and he called the name of the well Esek; because they strove with him. [Gen 26:20 KJV]And they digged another well, and strove for that also: and he called the name of it Sitnah. [Gen 26:21 KJV]And he removed from thence, and digged another well; and for that they strove not: and he called the name of it Rehoboth; and he said, For now the LORD hath made room for us, and we shall be fruitful in the land. [Gen 26:22 KJV]And he went up from thence to Beersheba. [Gen 26:23 KJV]

When Isaac dug the third well the herdmen did not try to take that one and he called in Rehoboth and said now the LORD has made room for us and we shall be fruitful in the land and that same night the LORD appeared unto him fear not for I am the God of Abraham, I am with you, I will bless you and I will multiply you for my servant Abraham's sake. This must have been comforting for Isaac because God had commanded him to stay in the land but the people of the land did not make that easy, however God did not promise easy, He promised to be with him, to bless him, to multiply him for his father Abraham's sake.

And the LORD appeared unto him the same night, and said, I [am] the God of Abraham thy father: fear not, for I [am] with thee, and will bless thee, and multiply thy seed for my servant Abraham's sake. [Gen 26:24 KJV]And he builded an altar there, and called upon the name of the LORD, and pitched his tent there: and there Isaac's servants digged a well. [Gen 26:25 KJV]

Abimelech went to Isaac to ask him not to harm them, he reminded Isaac that they had treated him well and had not touched him and had sent him away in peace. They wanted to make a covenant with Isaac because they realized that Isaac was blessed of the LORD and that God was with him. That same day Isaac servants came to him and said we have found water.

Why all of this attention to wells, it was the water in the wells that Isaac believed was going to cause them to be fruitful, how can we connect this to us today? There are many instances but we will use one that sums it all up in one verse **But whosoever drinketh of the water that I shall give him shall never thirst; but the water that I shall give him shall be in him a well of water springing up into everlasting life. [Jhn 4:14 KJV]** Jesus is taking to the woman at the well and the water from this well springs up into everlasting life, water that will cause you never to thirst again.

Then Abimelech went to him from Gerar, and Ahuzzath one of his friends, and Phichol the chief captain of his army. [Gen 26:26 KJV]And Isaac said unto them, Wherefore come ye to me, seeing ye hate me, and have sent me away from you? [Gen 26:27 KJV]And they said, We saw certainly that the LORD was with thee: and we said, Let there be now an oath betwixt us, [even] betwixt us and thee, and let us make a covenant with thee; [Gen 26:28 KJV]That thou wilt do us no hurt, as we have not touched thee, and as we have done unto thee nothing but good, and have sent thee away in peace: thou [art] now the blessed of the LORD. [Gen 26:29 KJV]And it came to pass the same day, that Isaac's servants came, and told him concerning the well which they had digged, and said unto him, We have found water. [Gen 26:32 KJV]And he called it Shebah: therefore the name of the city [is] Beersheba unto this day. [Gen 26:33 KJV]

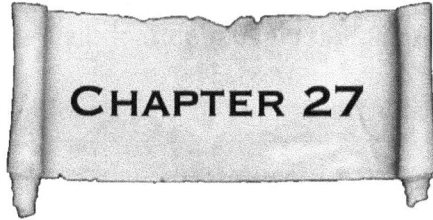

CHAPTER 27

ISAAC PASSES THE BLESSING TO HIS SON

This is the climax of the time of Jacob and Esau living together with their mother and father. Remember what God said to Rebekah when these twins were in her womb **"And the LORD said unto her, Two nations [are] in thy womb, and two manner of people shall be separated from thy bowels; and [the one] people shall be stronger than [the other] people; and the elder shall serve the younger." [Gen 25:23 KJV]** it is now time for this word to start the process of manifestation.

It is clear that Esau did not plan to follow the life that his family was accustomed to, he did not stay home to take care of sheep, he liked to hunt and that is what he spent time on, but how many know if you have to hunt for food you may be hungry sometimes. Esau also knew that his parents were following the directions that the LORD had given their parent Abraham and he went out to do something that he knew they did not approve of and that set the tone of his heart. He married a woman that his parents did not approve of:

And Esau was forty years old when he took to wife Judith the daughter of Beeri the Hittite, and Bashemath the daughter of Elon the Hittite: [Gen 26:34 KJV]Which were a grief of mind unto Isaac and to Rebekah. [Gen 26:35 KJV]

As we follow the story of what happens to these two brothers we can see the analogy of what the LORD had in mind regarding the first and the second Adam. One brother shall be stronger than the other and the older shall serve the younger. This is a theme that we can find in several places.

For instance the story of what happened with Ruben and Joseph the sons of Jacob, Ruben was the first born and should have received the double blessing, but he disrespected his father's bed and ended up being cursed instead of being blessed and that is what happened to the first Adam, he disobeyed his father and as a result we all have a sin nature passed down to us, another example is the sons of Tamar when the position of the first born was changed in the womb, the one that should have been second born the younger of the two changed his position in the womb and became the first born. A*nd it came to pass, as he drew back his hand, that, behold, his brother came out: and she said, How hast thou broken forth? [this] breach [be] upon thee: therefore his name was called*

Pharez. [Gen 38:29 KJV] and we see that is what the second Adam Jesus Christ did, He was the second Adam but the first born of the living.

Let's take a closer look at Isaac's desire to give the blessing to his first born son Esau:

And it came to pass, that when Isaac was old, and his eyes were dim, so that he could not see, he called Esau his eldest son, and said unto him, My son: and he said unto him, Behold, [here am] I. [Gen 27:1 KJV]And he said, Behold now, I am old, I know not the day of my death: [Gen 27:2 KJV]Now therefore take, I pray thee, thy weapons, thy quiver and thy bow, and go out to the field, and take me [some] venison; [Gen 27:3 KJV] And make me savoury meat, such as I love, and bring [it] to me, that I may eat; that my soul may bless thee before I die. [Gen 27:4 KJV]

Rebekah decided to trick Isaac into thinking that Jacob was Esau so that Isaac would give the blessing to Jacob. Now passing down the blessing was a little more difficult now because there were two sons and the blessing can only be given to one. Notice that neither Isaac nor Rebekah inquired of the LORD which one to give the blessing to; we know that they both knew how because of the relationship that was displayed by Isaac when Rebekah was barren and of Rebekah when the twins were fighting in her womb. In the end each wanted their favorite to get the blessing.

When Rebekah heard that Isaac sent Esau on a mission to prepare a meal for him to eat and then he would give him the blessing she devised a plan to make sure that Jacob gets the blessing. This was a very elaborate process but she was willing to do whatever it took to get that for Jacob.

Rebekah was told by God the older son would serve the younger and it does not say in the text that she shared that with Isaac or not because that may have influenced their efforts to move in this situation as they did. Since God had already said to Rebekah that the older would serve the younger that would be an indication that Jacob should be the one to receive the blessing.

Jacob was concerned about being cursed by his father, because he knew that Esau was a hairy man and that he was not and if caught he would be found to be a deceiver and be cursed instead of being blessed, but Rebekah said let your curse be on me.

Isaac was depending on his five senses instead of God to help him in this blessing process. Therefore when Jacob came to him pretending to be Esau he smelled the clothes, they smelled like Esau, he touched his skin and it was hairy like Esau, and he ate the food that Rebekah had cooked, it tasted like Esau's. Isaac did not hear the voice of Esau, he said your voice is that of Jacob but the hands are that of Esau. Jacob could not change his voice, but Isaac relied on his other senses and did not seriously question the voices not matching, therefore he blessed Jacob thinking that it was Esau. None of what Isaac thought was Esau was Esau and now Esau has nothing left. He had sold his birthright to Jacob and now Jacob has stolen his blessing. This is a lesson for us also, how many times have we listened to our own voice or the devils voice and followed that thinking that it was God?

And Rebekah heard when Isaac spake to Esau his son. And Esau went to the field to hunt [for] venison, [and] to bring [it]. [Gen 27:5 KJV]And Rebekah spake unto Jacob her son, saying, Behold, I heard thy father speak unto Esau thy brother, saying, [Gen 27:6 KJV]Bring me venison, and make me savoury meat, that I may eat, and bless thee before the LORD before my death. [Gen 27:7 KJV]Now therefore, my son, obey my voice according to that which I command thee. [Gen 27:8 KJV]Go now to the flock, and fetch me from thence two good kids of the goats; and I will make them savoury meat for thy father, such as he loveth: [Gen 27:9 KJV]And thou shalt bring [it] to thy father, that he may eat, and that he may bless thee before his death. [Gen 27:10 KJV]And Jacob said to Rebekah his mother, Behold, Esau my brother [is] a hairy man, and I [am] a smooth man: [Gen 27:11 KJV]My father peradventure will feel me, and I shall seem to him as a deceiver; and I shall bring a curse upon me, and not a blessing. [Gen 27:12 KJV]And his mother said unto him, Upon me [be] thy curse, my son: only obey my voice, and go fetch me [them]. [Gen 27:13 KJV]And he went, and fetched, and brought [them] to his mother: and his mother made savoury meat, such as his father loved. [Gen 27:14 KJV]And Rebekah took goodly raiment of her eldest son Esau, which [were] with her in the house, and put them upon Jacob her younger son: [Gen 27:15 KJV]And she put the skins of the kids of the goats upon his hands, and upon the smooth of his neck: [Gen 27:16 KJV]And she gave the savoury meat and the bread, which she had prepared, into the hand of her son Jacob. [Gen 27:17 KJV]And he came unto his father, and said, My father: and he said, Here [am] I; who [art] thou, my son? [Gen 27:18 KJV]And Jacob said unto his father, I [am] Esau thy firstborn; I have done according as thou badest me: arise, I pray thee, sit and eat of my venison, that thy soul may bless me. [Gen 27:19 KJV]And Isaac said unto his son, How [is it] that thou hast found [it] so quickly, my son? And he said, Because the LORD thy God brought [it] to me. [Gen 27:20 KJV]And Isaac said unto Jacob, Come near, I pray thee, that I may feel thee, my son, whether thou [be] my very son Esau or not. [Gen 27:21 KJV]And Jacob went near unto Isaac his father; and he felt him, and said, The voice [is] Jacob's voice, but the hands [are] the hands of Esau. [Gen 27:22 KJV]And he discerned him not, because his hands were hairy, as his brother Esau's hands: so he blessed him. [Gen 27:23 KJV]And he said, [Art] thou my very son Esau? And he said, I [am]. [Gen 27:24 KJV]And he said, Bring [it] near to me, and I will eat of my son's venison, that my soul may bless thee. And he brought [it] near to him, and he did eat: and he brought him wine, and he drank. [Gen 27:25 KJV]And his father Isaac said unto him, Come near now, and kiss me, my son. [Gen 27:26 KJV]

Before we go further let us take a look at Esau one more time. He dishonored his father, by marrying someone that he knew his father disapproved of, he preferred to not participate in the family business that God had given them to prosper them. God was not multiplying the animals of the field that Esau loved to go out and get, the inheritance had to do with taking care of the sheep, cattle, goats, camels, farming the land, planting the corn or grapes and whatever else Abraham had left for them to do. Jacob did that but Esau did not care about that at all. But he wants the responsibility to take care of activities that he despises. Abraham honored his father Terah, Isaac honored his father Abraham and Jacob honored his father Isaac by staying in place to take care of the family business and did not marry anyone that his father did not approve. That is true of us today, as believers we cannot spiritually marry anybody but the Lord Jesus Christ because He is the only one that our Father God Jehovah approves. Nor should we marry anybody naturally that God has not presented to us as a candidate.

Esau is still Jacobs's brother but his is not the one that God would use to keep his promise to Abraham. God used Esau as an example when he was talking to the priest in Malachi about not honoring Him as their Father, God said that he loved Jacob but He hated Esau and God also said if I be a father to you where is my honor. Take a look at what God said about Esau to the prophet Malachi *"The burden of the word of the LORD to Israel by Malachi. [Mal 1:1 KJV]I have loved you, saith the LORD. Yet ye say, Wherein hast thou loved us? [Was] not Esau Jacob's brother? saith the LORD: yet I loved Jacob, [Mal 1:2 KJV]And I hated Esau, and laid his mountains and his heritage waste for the dragons of the wilderness. [Mal 1:3 KJV]" A son honoureth [his] father, and a servant his master: if then I [be] a father, where [is] mine honour? and if I [be] a master, where [is] my fear? saith the LORD of hosts unto you, O priests, that despise my name. And ye say, Wherein have we despised thy name? [Mal 1:6 KJV]*

We can see from this passage how important it is to God to honor your natural and spiritual father. Esau did not honor either.

The Blessing is now passed on to Isaac's son Jacob and he is the one that the inheritance of Abraham would be passed down through.

Isaac blessed Jacob:
- God give thee the dew of the heaven and the fatness of the earth
- Plenty of corn and wine
- Let people serve thee
- And nations bow down to thee
- Be lord over thy brethren
- Let thy mother's sons bow down to thee
- Cursed be every one that curses you
- Blessed be he that bless thee

And he came near, and kissed him: and he smelled the smell of his raiment, and blessed him, and said, See, the smell of my son [is] as the smell of a field which the LORD hath blessed: [Gen 27:27 KJV]Therefore God give thee of the dew of heaven, and the fatness of the earth, and plenty of corn and wine: [Gen 27:28 KJV]Let people serve thee, and nations bow down to thee: be lord over thy brethren, and let thy mother's sons bow down to thee: cursed [be] every one that curseth thee, and blessed [be] he that blesseth thee. [Gen 27:29 KJV]

Now it is time to deal with the problem at hand, no one mentioned how Esau might take the news of his blessing be stolen by his brother, but as soon as he returns the pressure of dealing with this is at hand. When Esau returned to his father with the food that he sent him to get, he found out that his brother had stolen the blessing. Esau wept before his father and asked him is there at least one blessing left for me and Isaac said no, I have made him your lord and all of his brethren I have given him as servants, I have given him the corn and wine and there is nothing left for you, but this is what you can expect:

- I have made him your lord
- All his brethren I have given to him for servants
- With corn and wine have I sustained him
- Thy dwelling shall be the fatness of the earth and of the dew of heaven from above
- And by your sword shalt you live, and shalt serve your brother
- And it shall come to pass when you shalt have the dominion, that you shalt break his yoke from off your neck.

And it came to pass, as soon as Isaac had made an end of blessing Jacob, and Jacob was yet scarce gone out from the presence of Isaac his father, that Esau his brother came in from his hunting. [Gen 27:30 KJV] And he also had made savoury meat, and brought it unto his father, and said unto his father, Let my father arise, and eat of his son's venison, that thy soul may bless me. [Gen 27:31 KJV]And Isaac his father said unto him, Who [art] thou? And he said, I [am] thy son, thy firstborn Esau. [Gen 27:32 KJV]And Isaac trembled very exceedingly, and said, Who? where [is] he that hath taken venison, and brought [it] me, and I have eaten of all before thou camest, and have blessed him? yea, [and] he shall be blessed. [Gen 27:33 KJV]And when Esau heard the words of his father, he cried with a great and exceeding bitter cry, and said unto his father, Bless me, [even] me also, O my father. [Gen 27:34 KJV]And he said, Thy brother came with subtilty, and hath taken away thy blessing. [Gen 27:35 KJV]And he said, Is not he rightly named Jacob? for he hath supplanted me these two times: he took away my birthright; and, behold, now he hath taken away my blessing. And he said, Hast thou not reserved a blessing for me? [Gen 27:36 KJV]And Isaac answered and said unto Esau, Behold, I have made him thy lord, and all his brethren have I given to him for servants; and with corn and wine have I sustained him: and what shall I do now unto thee, my son? [Gen 27:37 KJV]And Esau said unto his father, Hast thou but one blessing, my father? bless me, [even] me also, O my father. And Esau lifted up his voice, and wept. [Gen 27:38 KJV]And Isaac his father answered and said unto him, Behold, thy dwelling shall be the fatness of the earth, and of the dew of heaven from above; [Gen 27:39 KJV]And by thy sword shalt thou live, and shalt serve thy brother; and it shall come to pass when thou shalt have the dominion, that thou shalt break his yoke from off thy neck. [Gen 27:40 KJV]

Esau hated his brother Jacob and purposed in his heart to kill him when his father died. This is interesting because that is what Cain purposed in his heart about his brother Abel. Esau had opportunity to do what Jacob did but he refused yet he wanted all that his brother had and that is also what Cain did, he had opportunity to do well before God but he did not want to do that.

This is a lesson for us today, when we see God blessing our brothers in Christ because they decided to live by faith and we are not ready to do that yet, or if we see that they forgive people quickly and we have not submitted to that word of God yet or if we see them practice love as Jesus did and we can't see that in our immediate future are we happy for them or do we murder them with the words from our mouth.

After hearing that Esau wanted to harm his brother **Rebekah called Jacob in and told him that his brother wanted to kill him and told him to go to her brother Laban in Haran and stay there a few days until Esau was over his anger and forgets what you did to him and she said that she would send for him when that happens.** Now she had to get Isaac to go along with the plan so she tells Isaac that Jacob should go to her brother's house to find a wife. Now Jacob has to leave the land of his inheritance to find a wife and to flee for his life.

It is interesting to note here that this is the last time Rebekah is mentioned as an active participant in family matters the next time she is mentioned will be her place of burial, she never came into the opportunity to send for Jacob and a few days tuned into twenty one years.

And Esau hated Jacob because of the blessing wherewith his father blessed him: and Esau said in his heart, The days of mourning for my father are at hand; then will I slay my brother Jacob. [Gen 27:41 KJV]And these words of Esau her elder son were told to Rebekah: and she sent and called Jacob her younger son, and said unto him, Behold, thy brother Esau, as touching thee, doth comfort himself, [purposing] to kill thee. [Gen 27:42 KJV]Now therefore, my son, obey my voice; and arise, flee thou to Laban my brother to Haran; [Gen 27:43 KJV] And tarry with him a few days, until thy brother's fury turn away; [Gen 27:44 KJV]Until thy brother's anger turn away from thee, and he forget [that] which thou hast done to him: then I will send, and fetch thee from thence: why should I be deprived also of you both in one day? [Gen 27:45 KJV]And Rebekah said to Isaac, I am weary of my life because of the daughters of Heth: if Jacob take a wife of the daughters of Heth, such as these [which are] of the daughters of the land, what good shall my life do me? [Gen 27:46 KJV]

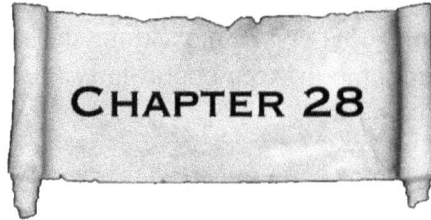

CHAPTER 28

JACOB

JACOBS'S LIFE CHAPTERS 28-35

Isaac calls Jacob into him and blessed him and sent him to Padanaram to the house of Bethuel to find a wife among his mother's people and from the daughters of his mother's brother Laban. Isaac blessed Jacob and said to him:

- God Almighty bless you
- Make thee Fruitful and multiply you
- That you may be a multitude of people
- And give you the blessing of Abraham to you and to thy seed with you
- And that you inherit the land wherein you are a stranger which God gave unto Abraham

And Isaac called Jacob, and blessed him, and charged him, and said unto him, Thou shalt not take a wife of the daughters of Canaan. [Gen 28:1 KJV]Arise, go to Padanaram, to the house of Bethuel thy mother's father; and take thee a wife from thence of the daughters of Laban thy mother's brother. [Gen 28:2 KJV]And God Almighty bless thee, and make thee fruitful, and multiply thee, that thou mayest be a multitude of people; [Gen 28:3 KJV]And give thee the blessing of Abraham, to thee, and to thy seed with thee; that thou mayest inherit the land wherein thou art a stranger, which God gave unto Abraham. [Gen 28:4 KJV]And Isaac sent away Jacob: and he went to Padanaram unto Laban, son of Bethuel the Syrian, the brother of Rebekah, Jacob's and Esau's mother. [Gen 28:5 KJV]

Jacob obeyed his father and his mother and left to go to his uncle Laban's house to find a wife. Jacob had to leave everything behind; all of the wealth that Isaac had would not be useful to him where he was going because he could not take very much with him. The text indicates that he only took himself; Esau was left behind with all of his father's wealth because Jacob is gone, and keeping all that in mind notice that Esau is still being disobedient to his father. When he found out that Isaac had blessed Jacob and sent him to find a wife and said to him what both boys already knew that they did not want them to marry any of the daughters of Canaan. When Esau saw that his parents were not pleased with their sons marrying the daughters of Canaan he went to Ishmael and took unto himself a wife from the people of Ishmael. That was not any better because remember his father and mother did not send him there, he did that on his own. Have you ever disobeyed the authority over you and did what you thought was best and later realized that action was still not approved even though you did not think it mattered? That is what happened to Esau, he did not value his parent's wisdom or authority.

When Esau saw that Isaac had blessed Jacob, and sent him away to Padanaram, to take him a wife from thence; and that as he blessed him he gave him a charge, saying, Thou shalt not take a wife of the daughters of Canaan; [Gen 28:6 KJV] And that Jacob obeyed his father and his mother, and was gone to Padanaram; [Gen 28:7 KJV]And Esau seeing that the daughters of Canaan pleased not Isaac his father; [Gen 28:8 KJV Then went Esau unto Ishmael, and took unto the wives which he had Mahalath the daughter of Ishmael Abraham's son, the sister of Nebajoth, to be his wife. [Gen 28:9 KJV]

Jacob started his journey and when night came he placed a stone under his head as a pillar and fell asleep and had a dream of a ladder set up on earth and the top of it reached heaven and the angels of God were ascending and descending on it and the LORD stood above it and said;

- I am the LORD God of Abraham your father and the God of Isaac
- The land whereon thou lie I will give it to you and your seed
- And your seed shall be as the dust of the earth
- You shall spread abroad to the west, to the east, to the north and south
- And in your seed shall all the families of the earth be blessed
- Behold I am with you and will keep you in all places where you go
- And I will bring you again into this land for I will not leave you until I have done that which I have spoken of you

Then Jacob said surely the LORD is in this place and I did not know it.

And Jacob went out from Beersheba, and went toward Haran. [Gen 28:10 KJV] And he lighted upon a certain place, and tarried there all night, because the sun was set; and he took of the stones of that place, and put [them for] his pillows, and lay down in that place to sleep. [Gen 28:11 KJV]And he dreamed, and behold a ladder set up on the earth, and the top of it reached to heaven: and behold the angels of God ascending and descending on it. [Gen 28:12 KJV]And, behold, the LORD stood above it, and said, I [am] the LORD God of Abraham thy father, and the God of Isaac: the land whereon thou liest, to thee will I give it, and to thy seed; [Gen 28:13 KJV]And thy seed shall be as the dust of the earth, and thou shalt spread abroad to the west, and to the east, and to the north, and to the south: and in thee and in thy seed shall all the families of the earth be blessed. [Gen 28:14 KJV]And, behold, I [am] with thee, and will keep thee in all [places] whither thou goest, and will bring thee again into this land; for I will not leave thee, until I have done [that] which I have spoken to thee of. [Gen 28:15 KJV]And Jacob awaked out of his sleep, and he said, Surely the LORD is in this place; and I knew [it] not. [Gen 28:16 KJV]

Jacob was afraid and he said this is an awesome place and this is the gate of heaven this is none other than the house of God and he called that place Bethel. He anointed the stone with oil and said this stone that I have set for a pillar shall be God's house, it was called Luz at first and he made a vow to the LORD. This was a part of his vow to God, he said to God, I will give you a tenth of all that you give me if you:

- Be with me and keep me in the way that I go
- And will give me bread to eat
- And clothes to put on
- So that I can come again to my father's house in peace
- Then shall the LORD be my God

And he was afraid, and said, How dreadful [is] this place! this [is] none other but the house of God, and this [is] the gate of heaven. [Gen 28:17 KJV]And Jacob rose up early in the morning, and took the stone that he had put [for] his pillows, and set it up [for] a pillar, and poured oil upon the top of it. [Gen 28:18 KJV]And he called the name of that place Bethel: but the name of that city [was called] Luz at the first. [Gen 28:19 KJV]And Jacob vowed a vow, saying, If God will be with me, and will keep me in this way that I go, and will give me bread to eat, and raiment to put on, [Gen 28:20 KJV]So that I come again to my father's house in peace; then shall the LORD be my God: [Gen 28:21 KJV]And this stone, which I have set [for] a pillar, shall be God's house: and of all that thou shalt give me I will surely give the tenth unto thee. [Gen 28:22 KJV]

CHAPTER 29

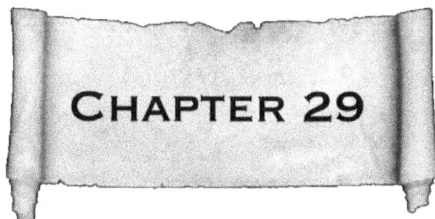

JACOB FINDS HIS WIFE

Jacob went on to the land of the people of the east and eventually saw Rachel the daughter of Laban his mother's brother. He kissed her and wept and told her that he was Rebekah's son and when Laban heard this news he ran to meet him. Laban invited him in and he stayed with them in the space of a month.

Remember, Jacob is not just getting away from his angry brother but he is also looking for a wife but he has not communicated that fact to his uncle yet. He did communicate much information to Laban but did not mention that he wanted to marry his daughter. Laban had two daughters Rachel the youngest was beautiful and Leah the oldest had weak eyes. Jacob loved Rachel, however it was customary for the older, first born daughter to marry first and it would have been easy for Laban to convey this to Jacob but he did not, because he was also a deceiver and we find that out as the text goes on to explain what happened.

Laban asked Jacob what would be the price for him to work for him and Jacob said, I will serve you seven years for Rachel, Jacob was willing to pay a large price for her, and Laban agreed to give him Rachel after the seven years were completed.

Then Jacob went on his journey, and came into the land of the people of the east. [Gen 29:1 KJV]And it came to pass, when Jacob saw Rachel the daughter of Laban his mother's brother, and the sheep of Laban his mother's brother, that Jacob went near, and rolled the stone from the well's mouth, and watered the flock of Laban his mother's brother. [Gen 29:10 KJV]And Jacob kissed Rachel, and lifted up his voice, and wept. [Gen 29:11 KJV]And Jacob told Rachel that he [was] her father's brother, and that he [was] Rebekah's son: and she ran and told her father. [Gen 29:12 KJV]And it came to pass, when Laban heard the tidings of Jacob his sister's son, that he ran to meet him, and embraced him, and kissed him, and brought him to his house. And he told Laban all these things. [Gen 29:13 KJV]And Laban said to him, Surely thou [art] my bone and my flesh. And he abode with him the space of a month. [Gen 29:14 KJV]And Laban said unto Jacob, Because thou [art] my brother, shouldest thou therefore serve me for nought? tell me, what [shall] thy wages [be]? [Gen 29:15 KJV]And Laban had two daughters: the name of the elder [was] Leah, and the name of the younger [was] Rachel. [Gen 29:16 KJV]Leah [was] tender eyed; but Rachel was beautiful and well favoured. [Gen 29:17 KJV]And Jacob loved Rachel; and said, I will serve thee seven years for Rachel thy younger daughter. [Gen 29:18 KJV]And Laban said, [It is] better that I give her to thee, than that I should give her to another man: abide with me. [Gen 29:19 KJV]

The seven years went by fast for Jacob and it seemed to be only a few days because his love for Rachel was great. Jacob went to Laban and asked for his wife and Laban made a feast for the marriage of his daughter, however Laban sent his daughter Leah to Jacob instead of Rachel. Jacob had been deceived by Laban and this was a new experience for him, he had always been the deceiver not the victim of deception. He was very angry with Laban, as his brother Esau had been with him. Now he knows what that feels like because not only did Laban deceive him he cheated him because Leah was not who he worked for. By now Laban is enjoying the blessing of the favor that is on Jacob's life because the LORD was with him. Laban quickly soothes Jacob by asking him to wait one week for Leah's sake and then he would give him Rachel if he would be willing to serve him another seven years and Jacob agreed.

And Jacob served seven years for Rachel; and they seemed unto him [but] a few days, for the love he had to her. [Gen 29:20 KJV]And Jacob said unto Laban, Give [me] my wife, for my days are fulfilled, that I may go in unto her. [Gen 29:21 KJV]And Laban gathered together all the men of the place, and made a feast. [Gen 29:22 KJV]And it came to pass in the evening, that he took Leah his daughter, and brought her to him; and he went in unto her. [Gen 29:23 KJV] And Laban gave unto his daughter Leah Zilpah his maid [for] an handmaid. [Gen 29:24 KJV]And it came to pass, that in the morning, behold, it [was] Leah: and he said to Laban, What [is] this thou hast done unto me? did not I serve with thee for Rachel? wherefore then hast thou beguiled me? [Gen 29:25 KJV]And Laban said, It must not be so done in our country, to give the younger before the firstborn. [Gen 29:26 KJV] Fulfil her week, and we will give thee this also for the service which thou shalt serve with me yet seven other years. [Gen 29:27 KJV] And Jacob did so, and fulfilled her week: and he gave him Rachel his daughter to wife also. [Gen 29:28 KJV]And Laban gave to Rachel his daughter Bilhah his handmaid to be her maid. [Gen 29:29 KJV]

It is going to take a little more deception in Jacob's life experiences in order for him to let that go and change his behavior of being a deceiver himself, but now he is content because Rachel makes life easy for him he loves her that much. He went in to Rachel more than to Leah and the LORD saw that she was hated and He opened her womb. This is tremendous to me because it must have been very difficult for Leah to get through the days when you knew that she was hated.

Since Leah was Jacob's wife, she was supposed to be loved, but she was not, this is not how a wife should experience a marriage, therefore God demonstrated the love He had for her by giving her a blessing to have children that would love her. In addition, God would later explain that the husband is to love his wife as Christ loves the church as His wife. Christ's love for the church, His bride is not based on any physical characteristics or performance. He has demonstrated this by being willing to pay the ultimate price of His physical life for our spiritual life, we could do nothing to deserve that, and He left no one out, all are included even the weak eyed, hardheaded and stiff-necked ones.

Leah however, did not use the children that were born first to her to comfort herself; she tried to use them to gain Jacob's love. However, when Jacob first saw Rachel he did not have children in mind, all he saw was a beautiful woman that he wanted, he was walking in the footsteps of his father and grandfather both of which married very beautiful women. The first born son was something that most men longed for in that time period but Jacob did not want that more than Rachel.

Leah said the LORD has looked upon my affliction and she bare a son and she named him *'behold, a son'* **Reuben** = behold, a son, in other words, look Jacob – a son surely you will love me now. This lets us know how important it is for people to know that they are loved, even the worst person will receive love. Leah gave birth to a second son and now she says because the Lord heard that I was hated He has given me this son and she named him *'heard'* - **Simeon** = heard, now she is still waiting on her husband Jacob to love her, but the LORD has demonstrated his love twice now and she is still not understanding. How did she know that the LORD *saw that* she was hated and gave her a son? How did she know that the LORD *heard about* her affliction and gave to her another son? The Bible does not say but we know that the LORD got the message to her and she had the correct information. She gave birth to a third son and said now this time my husband will be joined to me and she named him *'joined to'* - **Levi** = joined to, but that did not happen as she supposed. By now she understands that the LORD loves her but her husband does not love her as he loves Rachel, and having these sons for him has not changed that situation. Then Leah gave birth to a forth son and she named him *'praised'* **Judah** = praised and said now I will praise the LORD and she stopped having children. Let's take a look and the number four, it is symbolic of worldwide and universal, Leah has given birth to four of Jacobs sons and the fourth one Praise (**Judah**), will be in the bloodline of Jesus Christ.

And he went in also unto Rachel, and he loved also Rachel more than Leah, and served with him yet seven other years. [Gen 29:30 KJV]And when the LORD saw that Leah [was] hated, he opened her womb: but Rachel [was] barren. [Gen 29:31 KJV]And Leah conceived, and bare a son, and she called his name Reuben: for she said, Surely the LORD hath looked upon my affliction; now therefore my husband will love me. [Gen 29:32 KJV]And she conceived again, and bare a son; and said, Because the LORD hath heard that I [was] hated, he hath therefore given me this [son] also: and she called his name Simeon. [Gen 29:33 KJV]And she conceived again, and bare a son; and said, Now this time will my husband be joined unto me, because I have born him three sons: therefore was his name called Levi. [Gen 29:34 KJV]And she conceived again, and bare a son: and she said, Now will I praise the LORD: therefore she called his name Judah; and left bearing. [Gen 29:35 KJV]

CHAPTER 30

THE LORD MULTIPLIES JACOB

When Rachel saw that she had no children, she envied her sister and came up with a plan to help her compete with her sister to have children also. By now Jacob should have given her the information about the long period of time that his mother and grandmother had to wait before children were born to them. Rachel wanted children and she asked Jacob for them, he was trying but nothing was happening. He did not get the information from his father Isaac to pray for his barren wife instead he became angry when she demanded of him to give her children because he knew that was an action of the LORD. He said to her I am not God, who is able to withhold the fruit of the womb and her reply was to ask him to marry her maid, Bilhah and have children by her. He agreed. This is what her grandmother-in-law Sarah did and both men apparently were comfortable with that request. The first son that Bilhah had for Jacob for Rachel's sake was Dan. When Dan was born Rachel said God has judged me and also has heard my voice and she named him *'a judge'* - **Dan** = a judge. Bilhah conceived again and gave birth to a second son and Rachel said I have wrestled with my sister and named him *'wrestling'* - **Naphtali** = wrestling.

And when Rachel saw that she bare Jacob no children, Rachel envied her sister; and said unto Jacob, Give me children, or else I die. [Gen 30:1 KJV]And Jacob's anger was kindled against Rachel: and he said, [Am] I in God's stead, who hath withheld from thee the fruit of the womb? [Gen 30:2 KJV]And she said, Behold my maid Bilhah, go in unto her; and she shall bear upon my knees, that I may also have children by her. [Gen 30:3 KJV]And she gave him Bilhah her handmaid to wife: and Jacob went in unto her. [Gen 30:4 KJV]And Bilhah conceived, and bare Jacob a son. [Gen 30:5 KJV]And Rachel said, God hath judged me, and hath also heard my voice, and hath given me a son: therefore called she his name Dan. [Gen 30:6 KJV]And Bilhah Rachel's maid conceived again, and bare Jacob a second son. [Gen 30:7 KJV]And Rachel said, With great wrestlings have I wrestled with my sister, and I have prevailed: and she called his name Naphtali. [Gen 30:8 KJV]

Leah and Rachel are biological sisters yet they spent their entire married lives trying to be first in the life of one man by being the one wife that he wanted. But they did not realize that Jacob had two wives and they were both his wife.

Now when Leah saw that she was not having children, then she decided to compete with her sister and she took her maid Zilpah and asked him to marry her so that she could have more children by him and he agreed. When Zilpah gave birth to her first son Leah said, a troop cometh and she named him 'troop' - Gad = troop, Zilpah gave birth to a second son and Leah said happy am I for the daughters will call me blessed and she named him 'happy' - Asher = happy.

This is another incident where the love of God can be clearly seen, the maids Bilhah and Zilpah were truly blessed in this situation because they would never had the opportunity to get married and have children because they were permanent slaves. The LORD allowed them both to be married and between the two of them four of Jacob's sons were born. Now we see the number four again, these women have given birth to the second set of four sons to Jacob. This is amazing when you take the time to see how perfect everything that God does fits together.

When Leah saw that she had left bearing, she took Zilpah her maid, and gave her Jacob to wife. [Gen 30:9 KJV]And Zilpah Leah's maid bare Jacob a son. [Gen 30:10 KJV]And Leah said, A troop cometh: and she called his name Gad. [Gen 30:11 KJV]And Zilpah Leah's maid bare Jacob a second son. [Gen 30:12 KJV]And Leah said, Happy am I, for the daughters will call me blessed: and she called his name Asher. [Gen 30:13 KJV]

Leah is still trying to compete with her sister and when Reuben brought her some mandrakes Rachel wanted some of them. Mandrakes in the Hebrew is defined as 'love-apple' or as exciting sexual desire, and favoring procreation, this fertility plant was so important to Rachel that she was willing to bargain with her sister for it. Leah wanted the opportunity to have children with Jacob again and Rachel agreed. What is more important Leah went to Jacob and told him that she had purchased him and he agreed to go into her that night? God listened to Leah and she conceived.

Leah begans to have children again and she said God hath given me my hire, because I have given my maiden to my husband. Leah is acknowledging her willingness to allow her maid to be married to her husband is something that God is pleased with and she named him *'there is recompense'* - **Issachar** = there is recompense this is Jacob ninth son, then Leah conceived again and she said God hath endued me with a good dowry; now my husband will dwell with me and she named him *'exalted'*- **Zebulun** = exalted. This is Jacob's tenth son and Leah's sixth. After this son Leah gave birth to a girl, Jacob's only daughter and she named her *'judgment'* **Dinah** = judgment. What an unusual name to give to her only daughter and what a strange word to speak over her life. Notice, that Leah said nothing about this child nor did she mention God or anyone else.

And Reuben went in the days of wheat harvest, and found mandrakes in the field, and brought them unto his mother Leah. Then Rachel said to Leah, Give me, I pray thee, of thy son's mandrakes. [Gen 30:14 KJV]And she said unto her, [Is it] a small matter that thou hast taken my husband? and wouldest thou take away my son's mandrakes also? And Rachel said, Therefore he shall lie with thee to night for thy son's mandrakes. [Gen 30:15 KJV]And Jacob came out of the field in the evening, and Leah went out to meet him, and said, Thou must come in unto me; for surely I have hired thee with my son's mandrakes. And he lay with her that night. [Gen 30:16 KJV]And God hearkened unto Leah, and she conceived, and bare Jacob the fifth son. [Gen 30:17 KJV]And Leah said, God hath given me my hire, because I have given my maiden to my husband: and she called his name Issachar. [Gen 30:18 KJV]And Leah conceived again, and bare Jacob the sixth son. [Gen 30:19 KJV]And Leah said God hath endued me [with] a good dowry; now will my husband dwell with me, because I have born him six sons: and she called his name Zebulun. [Gen 30:20 KJV]And afterwards she bare a daughter, and called her name Dinah. [Gen 30:21 KJV]

God remembered Rachel and listened to her and opened her womb, she gave birth to a son and she said God hath taken away my reproach and the LORD shall add to me another son and she named him 'Jehovah has added' - Joseph = Jehovah has added.

And God remembered Rachel, and God hearkened to her, and opened her womb. [Gen 30:22 KJV]And she conceived, and bare a son; and said, God hath taken away my reproach: [Gen 30:23 KJV]And she called his name Joseph; and said, The LORD shall add to me another son. [Gen 30:24 KJV]

After Joseph was born, Jacob went to Laban and asked to leave with his wives and children whom he had served for, but Laban asked him to stay because he knew that God blessed him for Jacob's sake. Laban asked Jacob what he wanted to be paid and Jacob said to him, you know how little you had before I came and now it has increased unto a multitude and the LORD has blessed thee since my coming and now I must provide for my own house then Laban replied what shall I give you and Jacob said you will give me nothing but do this for me and I will feed and keep your flock - **I shall pass through all thy flock to day, removing from thence all the speckled and spotted cattle, and all the brown cattle among the sheep, and the spotted and speckled among the goats: and [of such] shall be my hire. So shall my righteousness answer for me in time to come, when it shall come for my hire before thy face: every one that is not speckled and spotted among the goats, and brown among the sheep, that shall be counted stolen with me.**

Laban agreed, but he removed that day the he goats that were ringstraked and spotted, and all the she goats that were speckled and spotted, and every one that had some white in it, and all the brown among the sheep, and gave them into the hand of his sons. And he set three days' journey between himself and Jacob: and Jacob fed the rest of Laban's flocks. This is a lesson for us today nobody can open doors that the LORD shuts and nobody can close the doors that He opens. Laban was wasting his time trying to outsmart Jacob because the LORD was with Jacob just as He is with us.

And it came to pass, when Rachel had born Joseph, that Jacob said unto Laban, Send me away, that I may go unto mine own place, and to my country. [Gen 30:25 KJV]Give [me] my wives and my children, for whom I have served thee, and let me go: for thou knowest my service which I have done thee. [Gen 30:26 KJV]And Laban said unto him, I pray thee, if I have found favour in thine eyes, [tarry: for] I have learned by experience that the LORD hath blessed me for thy sake. [Gen 30:27 KJV]And he said, Appoint me thy wages, and I will give [it]. [Gen 30:28 KJV]And he said unto him, Thou knowest how I have served thee, and how thy cattle was with me. [Gen 30:29 KJV]For [it was] little which thou hadst before I [came], and it is [now] increased unto a multitude; and the LORD hath blessed thee since my coming: and now when shall I provide for mine own house also? [Gen 30:30 KJV]And he said, What shall I give thee? And Jacob said, Thou shalt not give me any thing: if thou wilt do this thing for me, I will again feed [and] keep thy flock: [Gen 30:31 KJV]I will pass through all thy flock to day, removing from thence all the speckled and spotted cattle, and all the brown cattle among the sheep, and the spotted and speckled among the goats: and [of such] shall be my hire. [Gen 30:32 KJV]So shall my righteousness answer for me in time to come, when it shall come for my hire before thy face: every one that [is] not speckled and spotted among the goats, and brown among the sheep, that shall be counted stolen with me. [Gen 30:33 KJV]And Laban said, Behold, I would it might be according to thy word. [Gen 30:34 KJV]And he removed that day the he goats that were ringstraked and spotted, and all the she goats that were speckled and spotted, [and] every one that had [some] white in it, and all the brown among the sheep, and gave [them] into the hand of his sons. [Gen 30:35 KJV]And he set three days' journey betwixt himself and Jacob: and Jacob fed the rest of Laban's flocks. [Gen 30:36 KJV]

• Jacob received super natural help for God. Notice what Jacob did:

And Jacob took him rods of green poplar, and of the hazel and chesnut tree; and pilled white strakes in them, and made the white appear which [was] in the rods. [Gen 30:37 KJV]And he set the rods which he had pilled before the flocks in the gutters in the watering troughs when the flocks came to drink, that they should conceive when they came to drink. [Gen 30:38 KJV]And the flocks conceived before the rods, and brought forth cattle ringstraked, speckled, and spotted. [Gen 30:39 KJV]And Jacob did separate the lambs, and set the faces of the flocks toward the ringstraked, and all the brown in the flock of Laban; and he put his own flocks by themselves, and put them not unto Laban's cattle. [Gen 30:40 KJV]And it came to pass, whensoever the stronger cattle did conceive, that Jacob laid the rods before the eyes of the cattle in the gutters, that they might conceive among the rods. [Gen 30:41 KJV]But when the cattle were feeble, he put [them] not in: so the feebler were Laban's, and the stronger Jacob's. [Gen 30:42 KJV]And the man increased exceedingly, and had much cattle, and maidservants, and menservants, and camels, and asses. [Gen 30:43 KJV]

Jacob increased exceedingly in his family and he had many cattle, maidservants, menservants, camels, and asses.

CHAPTER 31

JACOB RETURNS TO HIS FATHER'S HOUSE

Once Laban's sons saw how the LORD was increasing Jacob they began to say that Jacob had taken away all that was their father's and Jacob saw that Laban's countenance had changed toward him and the LORD said to him it is time to return unto the land of your fathers and your kindred and I will be with you.

Jacob called Rachel and Leah to the field unto his flock and said unto them, I see your father's countenance, that it is not toward me as before; but the God of my father hath been with me and ye know that with all my power I have served your father. And your father hath deceived me, and changed my wages ten times; but God suffered him not to hurt me. If he said thus, the speckled shall be thy wages; then all the cattle bare speckled: and if he said thus, the ringstraked shall be thy hire; then bare all the cattle ringstraked. Thus God hath taken away the cattle of your father, and given them to me. And it came to pass at the time that the cattle conceived, that I lifted up mine eyes, and saw in a dream, and, behold, the rams which leaped upon the cattle were ringstraked, speckled, and grisled.

And he heard the words of Laban's sons, saying, Jacob hath taken away all that [was] our father's; and of [that] which [was] our father's hath he gotten all this glory. [Gen 31:1 KJV]And Jacob beheld the countenance of Laban, and, behold, it [was] not toward him as before. [Gen 31:2 KJV]And the LORD said unto Jacob, Return unto the land of thy fathers, and to thy kindred; and I will be with thee. [Gen 31:3 KJV]And Jacob sent and called Rachel and Leah to the field unto his flock, [Gen 31:4 KJV]And said unto them, I see your father's countenance, that it [is] not toward me as before; but the God of my father hath been with me. [Gen 31:5 KJV]And ye know that with all my power I have served your father. [Gen 31:6 KJV]And your father hath deceived me, and changed my wages ten times; but God suffered him not to hurt me. [Gen 31:7 KJV]If he said thus, The speckled shall be thy wages; then all the cattle bare speckled: and if he said thus, The ringstraked shall be thy hire; then bare all the cattle ringstraked. [Gen 31:8 KJV]Thus God hath taken away the cattle of your father, and given [them] to me. [Gen 31:9 KJV]And it came to pass at the time that the cattle conceived, that I lifted up mine eyes, and saw in a dream, and, behold, the rams which leaped upon the cattle [were] ringstraked, speckled, and grisled. [Gen 31:10 KJV]

Then Jacob said to them the angel of God spoke to me in a dream and said for me to lift my eyes and see all the rams that leap upon the cattle are ringstraked, speckled, and grisled for I have seen all that Laban doeth unto you, I am the God of Bethel where you anointed the pillar and where you vowed a vow unto men now arise and get out from this land and return unto the land of your kindred. Rachel and Leah agreed with Jacob and they prepared to leave but Rachel stole her father's images.

And the angel of God spake unto me in a dream, [saying], Jacob: And I said, Here [am] I. [Gen 31:11 KJV]And he said, Lift up now thine eyes, and see, all the rams which leap upon the cattle [are] ringstraked, speckled, and grisled: for I have seen all that Laban doeth unto thee. [Gen 31:12 KJV]I [am] the God of Bethel, where thou anointedst the pillar, [and] where thou vowedst a vow unto me: now arise, get thee out from this land, and return unto the land of thy kindred. [Gen 31:13 KJV]And Rachel and Leah answered and said unto him, [Is there] yet any portion or inheritance for us in our father's house? [Gen 31:14 KJV]Are we not counted of him strangers? for he hath sold us, and hath quite devoured also our money. [Gen 31:15 KJV]For all the riches which God hath taken from our father, that [is] ours, and our children's: now then, whatsoever God hath said unto thee, do. [Gen 31:16 KJV]Then Jacob rose up, and set his sons and his wives upon camels; [Gen 31:17 KJV]And he carried away all his cattle, and all his goods which he had gotten, the cattle of his getting, which he had gotten in Padanaram, for to go to Isaac his father in the land of Canaan. [Gen 31:18 KJV]And Laban went to shear his sheep: and Rachel had stolen the images that [were] her father's. [Gen 31:19 KJV]

Jacob left and headed toward Gilead without telling Laban and he had been gone three days before Laban found out about Jacob's leaving and he took his brethren and went after Jacob but God came to Laban the Syrian in a dream by night, and said unto him, Take heed that thou speak not to Jacob either good or bad. Laban wanted to know why Jacob left without telling him because he may have given him a going away party and Jacob replied I thought that you would take your daughters from me, then Laban ask him why did you steal my gods, then Jacob said to Laban whoever has your gods let him not live, Jacob did not know it was Rachel that had stolen them and the person that he had said should not live was the person that he loved the most. Jacobs's words concerning this matter would not fall to the ground. Laban searched everywhere, but Rachel was able to hide the gods from her father.

And Jacob stole away unawares to Laban the Syrian, in that he told him not that he fled. [Gen 31:20 KJV]So he fled with all that he had; and he rose up, and passed over the river, and set his face [toward] the mount Gilead. [Gen 31:21 KJV] And it was told Laban on the third day that Jacob was fled. [Gen

31:22 KJV]And he took his brethren with him, and pursued after him seven days' journey; and they overtook him in the mount Gilead. [Gen 31:23 KJV] And God came to Laban the Syrian in a dream by night, and said unto him, Take heed that thou speak not to Jacob either good or bad. [Gen 31:24 KJV] Then Laban overtook Jacob. Now Jacob had pitched his tent in the mount: and Laban with his brethren pitched in the mount of Gilead. [Gen 31:25 KJV] And Laban said to Jacob, What hast thou done, that thou hast stolen away unawares to me, and carried away my daughters, as captives [taken] with the sword? [Gen 31:26 KJV]Wherefore didst thou flee away secretly, and steal away from me; and didst not tell me, that I might have sent thee away with mirth, and with songs, with tabret, and with harp? [Gen 31:27 KJV]And hast not suffered me to kiss my sons and my daughters? thou hast now done foolishly in [so] doing. [Gen 31:28 KJV]It is in the power of my hand to do you hurt: but the God of your father spake unto me yesternight, saying, Take thou heed that thou speak not to Jacob either good or bad. [Gen 31:29 KJV]And now, [though] thou wouldest needs be gone, because thou sore longedst after thy father's house, [yet] wherefore hast thou stolen my gods? [Gen 31:30 KJV]And Jacob answered and said to Laban, Because I was afraid: for I said, Peradventure thou wouldest take by force thy daughters from me. [Gen 31:31 KJV]With whomsoever thou findest thy gods, let him not live: before our brethren discern thou what [is] thine with me, and take [it] to thee.

After Laban finished his search and did not find the images. Jacob was angry with him and said you searched all my stuff, what hast thou found of all thy household stuff? Set it here before my brethren and thy brethren that they may judge betwixt us both. Jacob did not know that Rachel had stolen the idols. Jacob asked him what is my trespass? What is my sin that thou hast so hotly pursued after me? I have been with you twenty years your ewes nor your she goats have not lost their young, and I have not eaten any of your flock, those that were torn of beasts I took the loss of it; of my hand didst thou require it, whether stolen by day, or stolen by night. I was; in the day the drought consumed me, and the frost by night; and my sleep departed from mine eyes. I served thee fourteen years for thy two daughters, and six years for thy cattle: and thou hast changed my wages ten times. Except the God of my father, the God of Abraham, and the fear of Isaac, had been with me, surely thou have sent me away now empty. God hath seen mine affliction and the labor of my hands, and rebuked you last night.

For Jacob knew not that Rachel had stolen them. [Gen 31:32 KJV]And Laban went into Jacob's tent, and into Leah's tent, and into the two maidservants' tents; but he found [them] not. Then went he out of Leah's tent, and entered into Rachel's tent. [Gen 31:33 KJV]Now Rachel had taken the images, and put them in the camel's furniture, and sat upon them. And Laban searched all the tent, but found [them] not. [Gen 31:34 KJV]And she said to her father, Let it not displease my lord that I cannot rise up before thee; for the custom of women [is] upon me. And he searched, but found not the images. [Gen 31:35 KJV]And Jacob was wroth, and chode with Laban: and Jacob answered and said to Laban, What [is] my trespass? what [is] my sin, that thou hast so hotly pursued after me? [Gen 31:36 KJV] Whereas thou hast searched all my stuff, what hast thou found of all thy household stuff? set [it] here before my brethren and thy brethren, that they may judge betwixt us both. [Gen 31:37 KJV]This twenty years [have] I [been] with thee; thy ewes and thy she goats have not cast their young, and the rams of thy flock have I not eaten. [Gen 31:38 KJV]That which was torn [of beasts] I brought not unto thee; I bare the loss of it; of my hand didst thou require it, [whether] stolen by day, or stolen by night. [Gen 31:39 KJV][Thus] I was; in the day the drought consumed me, and the frost by night; and my sleep departed from mine eyes. [Gen 31:40 KJV]Thus have I been twenty years in thy house; I served thee fourteen years for thy two daughters, and six years for thy cattle: and thou hast changed my wages ten times. [Gen 31:41 KJV]Except the God of my father, the God of Abraham, and the fear of Isaac, had been with me, surely thou hadst sent me away now empty. God hath seen mine affliction and the labour of my hands, and rebuked [thee] yesternight. [Gen 31:42 KJV]

Laban Answered Jacob and said these are my daughters, my children, and my cattle and let us make a covenant between us that you will not harm my daughters nor will you marry any other woman. **They made the covenant between them then Jacob offered sacrifice upon the mount, and called his brethren to eat bread: and they did eat bread, and tarried all night in the mount. When morning came Laban kissed his sons and daughters and blessed them and left.**

And Laban answered and said unto Jacob, [These] daughters [are] my daughters, and [these] children [are] my children, and [these] cattle [are] my cattle, and all that thou seest [is] mine: and what can I do this day unto these my daughters, or unto their children which they have born? [Gen 31:43 KJV] Now therefore come thou, let us make a covenant, I and thou; and let it be for a witness between me and thee. [Gen 31:44 KJV]And Jacob took a stone, and set it up [for] a pillar. [Gen 31:45 KJV]And Jacob said unto his brethren, Gather stones; and they took stones, and made an heap: and they did eat there upon the heap. [Gen 31:46 KJV]And Laban called it Jegarsahadutha: but Jacob called it Galeed. [Gen 31:47 KJV]And Laban said, This heap [is] a witness between me and thee this day. Therefore was the name of it called Galeed; [Gen 31:48 KJV] And Mizpah; for he said, The LORD watch between me and thee, when we are absent one from another. [Gen 31:49 KJV]If thou shalt afflict my daughters, or if thou shalt take [other] wives beside my daughters, no man [is] with us; see, God [is] witness betwixt me and thee. [Gen 31:50 KJV]And Laban said to Jacob, Behold this heap, and behold [this] pillar, which I have cast betwixt me and thee; [Gen 31:51 KJV]This heap [be] witness, and [this] pillar [be] witness, that I will not pass over this heap to thee, and that thou shalt not pass over this heap and this pillar unto me, for harm. [Gen 31:52 KJV]The God of Abraham, and the God of Nahor, the God of their father, judge betwixt us. And Jacob sware by the fear of his father Isaac. [Gen 31:53 KJV]Then Jacob offered sacrifice upon the mount, and called his brethren to eat bread: and they did eat bread, and tarried all night in the mount. [Gen 31:54 KJV]And early in the morning Laban rose up, and kissed his sons and his daughters, and blessed them: and Laban departed, and returned unto his place. [Gen 31:55 KJV]

CHAPTER 32

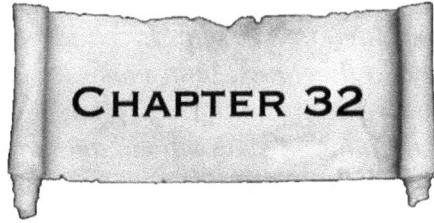

JACOB GET A NAME CHANGE

Jacob went on his way and the angels of God met him and he saw them, then he sent a message to Esau his brother in the land of Seir in Edom, he told them to tell him that he had been with their uncle Laban all this time and he now has oxen, asses, flocks and menservants and women servants and I am asking for grace in your sight.

The servants returned with a message that Esau was coming to meet him with four hundred men with him then Jacob was afraid. That is what we do today, even when God tells us to go forth some of us are fearful and will not go. Jacob prays to the LORD asking for help, he reminded God that he has told him to go and he is asking for His help. Then Jacob took two hundred she goats, and twenty he goats, two hundred ewes, and twenty rams, thirty camels with their colts, forty kine, and ten bulls, twenty she asses, and ten foals and gave them to his servants to take to Esau and tell him that it is a gift from Jacob.

And Jacob went on his way, and the angels of God met him. [Gen 32:1 KJV] And when Jacob saw them, he said, This [is] God's host: and he called the name of that place Mahanaim. [Gen 32:2 KJV]And Jacob sent messengers before him to Esau his brother unto the land of Seir, the country of Edom. [Gen 32:3 KJV] And he commanded them, saying, Thus shall ye speak unto my lord Esau; Thy servant Jacob saith thus, I have sojourned with Laban, and stayed there until now: [Gen 32:4 KJV]And I have oxen, and asses, flocks, and menservants, and womenservants: and I have sent to tell my lord, that I may find grace in thy sight. [Gen 32:5 KJV]And the messengers returned to Jacob, saying, We came to thy brother Esau, and also he cometh to meet thee, and four hundred men with him. [Gen 32:6 KJV]Then Jacob was greatly afraid and distressed: and he divided the people that [was] with him, and the flocks, and herds, and the camels, into two bands; [Gen 32:7 KJV]And said, If Esau come to the one company, and smite it, then the other company which is left shall escape. [Gen 32:8 KJV]And Jacob said, O God of my father Abraham, and God of my father Isaac, the LORD which saidst unto me, Return unto thy country, and to thy kindred, and I will deal well with thee: [Gen 32:9 KJV]I am not worthy of the least of all the mercies, and of all the truth, which thou hast shewed unto thy servant; for with my staff I passed over this Jordan; and now I am become two bands. [Gen 32:10 KJV]Deliver me, I pray thee, from the hand of my brother, from the hand of Esau: for I fear him, lest he will come and smite me, [and] the mother with the children. [Gen 32:11 KJV]And thou saidst, I will surely do thee good, and make thy seed as the sand of the sea, which cannot be numbered for multitude. [Gen 32:12 KJV]And he lodged there that same night; and took of that which came to his hand a present for Esau his brother; [Gen 32:13 KJV]Two hundred she goats, and twenty he goats, two hundred ewes, and twenty rams, [Gen 32:14 KJV]Thirty milch camels with their colts, forty kine, and ten bulls, twenty she asses, and ten foals. [Gen 32:15 KJV]And he delivered [them] into the hand of his servants, every drove by themselves; and said unto his servants, Pass over before me, and put a space betwixt drove and drove. [Gen 32:16 KJV]And he commanded the foremost, saying, When Esau my brother meeteth thee, and asketh thee, saying, Whose [art] thou? and whither goest thou? and whose [are] these before thee? [Gen 32:17 KJV]Then thou shalt say, [They be] thy servant Jacob's; it [is] a present sent unto my lord Esau: and, behold, also he [is] behind us. [Gen 32:18 KJV]And so commanded he the second, and the third, and all that followed the droves, saying, On this manner shall ye speak unto Esau, when ye find him. [Gen 32:19 KJV]And say ye moreover, Behold, thy servant Jacob [is] behind us. For he said, I will appease him with the present that goeth before me, and afterward I will see his face; peradventure he will accept of me. [Gen 32:20 KJV] So went the present over before him: and himself lodged that night in the company. [Gen 32:21 KJV]

Jacob sent his wives and his two women servants ahead of him and he stayed back alone and there he wrestled a man with him until the breaking of the day and when he saw that he prevailed not against him, he touched the hollow of his thigh and the hollow of his thigh was out of joint and he said to Jacob let me go for day breaketh and Jacob said I will not let you go until you bless me and he said unto him, what is your name and Jacob said Jacob And he said, **Thy name shall be called no more Jacob, but Israel - Israel = 'God prevails': for as a prince hast thou power with God and with men, and hast prevailed. And Jacob asked him, and said, tell me your name. And he said, why do you ask my name? And he blessed him there.** And Jacob called the name of the place Peniel: for I have seen God face to face and my life is preserved.

And he rose up that night, and took his two wives, and his two women servants, and his eleven sons, and passed over the ford Jabbok. [Gen 32:22 KJV]And he took them, and sent them over the brook, and sent over that he had. [Gen 32:23 KJV]And Jacob was left alone; and there wrestled a man with him until the breaking of the day. [Gen 32:24 KJV]And when he saw that he prevailed not against him, he touched the hollow of his thigh; and the hollow of Jacob's thigh was out of joint, as he wrestled with him. [Gen 32:25 KJV]And he said, Let me go, for the day breaketh. And he said, I will not let thee go, except thou bless me. [Gen 32:26 KJV]And he said unto him, What [is] thy name? And he said, Jacob. [Gen 32:27 KJV]And he said, Thy name shall be called no more Jacob, but Israel: for as a prince hast thou power with God and with men, and hast prevailed. [Gen 32:28 KJV]And Jacob asked [him], and said, Tell [me], I pray thee, thy name. And he said, Wherefore [is] it [that] thou dost ask after my name? And he blessed him there. [Gen 32:29 KJV]And Jacob called the name of the place Peniel: for I have seen God face to face, and my life is preserved. [Gen 32:30 KJV]And as he passed over Penuel the sun rose upon him, and he halted upon his thigh. [Gen 32:31 KJV]Therefore the children of Israel eat not [of] the sinew which shrank, which [is] upon the hollow of the thigh, unto this day: because he touched the hollow of Jacob's thigh in the sinew that shrank. [Gen 32:32 KJV]

CHAPTER 33

JACOB REUNITED WITH HIS BROTHER ESAU

Jacob looked and saw Esau and he divided his family, he put the two handmaids and their children in front, Leah and her children next and Rachel and Joseph last then he came to the front and bowed down to his brother and Esau ran to meet him, and embraced him, and fell on his neck, and kissed him: and they wept. **Esau offered to help him get back with him but Jacob said that the trip would be too harsh for the children and he purchased some land and pithed his tent in Shechem, which is in the land of Canaan, God told him to go back to the land of his father and kindred but he stopped in Shechem, he did not continue as he had said to Esau that he needed to travel slow because of the children.**

And Jacob lifted up his eyes, and looked, and, behold, Esau came, and with him four hundred men. And he divided the children unto Leah, and unto Rachel, and unto the two handmaids. [Gen 33:1 KJV]And he put the handmaids and their children foremost, and Leah and her children after, and Rachel and Joseph hindermost. [Gen 33:2 KJV]And he passed over before them, and bowed himself to the ground seven times, until he came near to his brother. [Gen 33:3 KJV] And Esau ran to meet him, and embraced him, and fell on his neck, and kissed him: and they wept. [Gen 33:4 KJV]And he lifted up his eyes, and saw the women and the children; and said, Who [are] those with thee? And he said, The children which God hath graciously given thy servant. [Gen 33:5 KJV] Then the handmaidens came near, they and their children, and they bowed themselves. [Gen 33:6 KJV]And Leah also with her children came near, and bowed themselves: and after came Joseph near and Rachel, and they bowed themselves. [Gen 33:7 KJV]And he said, What [meanest] thou by all this drove which I met? And he said, [These are] to find grace in the sight of my lord. [Gen 33:8 KJV]And Esau said, I have enough, my brother; keep that thou hast unto thyself. [Gen 33:9 KJV]And Jacob said, Nay, I pray thee, if now I have found grace in thy sight, then receive my present at my hand: for therefore I have seen thy face, as though I had seen the face of God, and thou wast pleased with me. [Gen 33:10 KJV]Take, I pray thee, my blessing that is brought to thee; because God hath dealt graciously with me, and because I have enough. And he urged him, and he took [it]. [Gen 33:11 KJV]And he said, Let us take our journey, and let us go, and I will go before thee. [Gen 33:12 KJV]And he said unto him, My lord knoweth that the children [are] tender, and the flocks and herds with young [are] with me: and if men should overdrive them one day, all the flock will die. [Gen 33:13 KJV]Let my lord, I pray thee, pass over before his servant: and I will lead on softly, according as the cattle that goeth before me and the children be able to endure, until I come unto my lord unto Seir. [Gen 33:14 KJV] And Esau said, Let me now leave with thee [some] of the folk that [are] with me. And he said, What needeth it? let me find grace in the sight of my lord. [Gen 33:15 KJV]So Esau returned that day on his way unto Seir. [Gen 33:16 KJV] And Jacob journeyed to Succoth, and built him an house, and made booths for his cattle: therefore the name of the place is called Succoth. [Gen 33:17 KJV] And Jacob came to Shalem, a city of Shechem, which [is] in the land of Canaan, when he came from Padanaram; and pitched his tent before the city. [Gen 33:18 KJV]And he bought a parcel of a field, where he had spread his tent, at the hand of the children of Hamor, Shechem's father, for an hundred pieces of money. [Gen 33:19 KJV]And he erected there an altar, and called it Elelohe-Israel. [Gen 33:20 KJV]

CHAPTER 34

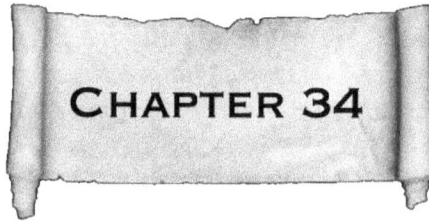

JACOB AT SHECHEM

Dinah the daughter of Leah, went out to see the daughters of the land. And when Shechem the son of Hamor the Hivite, prince of the country, saw her, he took her, and lay with her, and defiled her. And his soul clave unto Dinah the daughter of Jacob, and he loved the damsel, and spake kindly unto the damsel. Hamor wanted to marry her. Jacob heard what had happened to her and held his peace until his son came home from the field.

And Dinah the daughter of Leah, which she bare unto Jacob, went out to see the daughters of the land. [Gen 34:1 KJV]And when Shechem the son of Hamor the Hivite, prince of the country, saw her, he took her, and lay with her, and defiled her. [Gen 34:2 KJV]And his soul clave unto Dinah the daughter of Jacob, and he loved the damsel, and spake kindly unto the damsel. [Gen 34:3 KJV]And Shechem spake unto his father Hamor, saying, Get me this damsel to wife. [Gen 34:4 KJV]And Jacob heard that he had defiled Dinah his daughter: now his sons were with his cattle in the field: and Jacob held his peace until they were come. [Gen 34:5 KJV]And Hamor the father of Shechem went out unto Jacob to commune with him. [Gen 34:6 KJV]And the sons of Jacob came out of the field when they heard [it]: and the men were grieved, and they were very wroth, because he had wrought folly in Israel in lying with Jacob's daughter; which thing ought not to be done. [Gen 34:7 KJV]And Hamor communed with them, saying, The soul of my son Shechem longeth for your daughter: I pray you give her him to wife. [Gen 34:8 KJV]And make ye marriages with us, [and] give your daughters unto us, and take our daughters unto you. [Gen 34:9 KJV]

Dinah's brothers devised a plan to kill all the men in that city for dishonoring their sister. They deceived Shechem, when he asked for the dowry they required to give him Dinah for a wife. They never intended to give her as a wife nor did they have the authority to do so. They usurped the authority of their father Jacob, who had not given them permission to speak for him or avenge his daughter for him. They were in disobedience and rebellion and they were comfortable in doing this. However, they did have to deal with this later. They convinced the men to agree to be circumcised as a condition to get Dinah and they agreed. Once the men were all circumcised none of them were able to fight then Simeon and Levi, Dinah's brothers, took each man his sword, and came upon the city boldly, and slew all the males. And they slew Hamor and Shechem his son with the edge of the sword, and took Dinah out of Shechem's house, and went out. And Jacob said to Simeon and Levi, you have troubled me to make me to stink among the inhabitants of the land, among the Canaanites and the Perizzites: and I being few in number, they shall gather themselves together against me, and slay me; and I shall be destroyed, I and my house. And they said, Should he deal with our sister as with a harlot? They did not honor their father nor were they interested in what he thought. Many times we do things like this to people who are in authority over us. It does not matter who, it may be parents, or a boss, or the leader of a group spiritually or naturally and we do not realize the purpose of people that God has put in authority. The purpose is to bless you to speak over your life, to do you good, to take care of things on your behalf and that is very important to each of us so we want to make sure we recognize and honor God's authority.

And ye shall dwell with us: and the land shall be before you; dwell and trade ye therein, and get you possessions therein. [Gen 34:10 KJV]And Shechem said unto her father and unto her brethren, Let me find grace in your eyes, and what ye shall say unto me I will give. [Gen 34:11 KJV]Ask me never so much dowry and gift, and I will give according as ye shall say unto me: but give me the damsel to wife. [Gen 34:12 KJV]And the sons of Jacob answered Shechem and Hamor his father deceitfully, and said, because he had defiled Dinah their sister: [Gen 34:13 KJV]And they said unto them, We cannot do this thing, to give our sister to one that is uncircumcised; for that [were] a reproach unto us: [Gen 34:14 KJV]But in this will we consent unto you: If ye will be as we [be], that every male of you be circumcised; [Gen 34:15 KJV]Then will we give our daughters unto you, and we will take your daughters to us, and we will dwell with you, and we will become one people. [Gen 34:16 KJV]But if ye will not hearken unto us, to be circumcised; then will we take our daughter, and we will be gone. [Gen 34:17 KJV]And their words pleased Hamor, and Shechem Hamor's son. [Gen 34:18 KJV]And the young man deferred not to do the thing, because he had delight in Jacob's daughter: and he [was] more honorable than all the house of his father. [Gen 34:19 KJV]And Hamor and Shechem his son came unto the gate of their city, and communed with the men of their city, saying, [Gen 34:20 KJV]These men [are] peaceable with us; therefore let them dwell in the land, and trade therein; for the land, behold, [it is] large enough for them; let us take their daughters to us for wives, and let us give them our daughters. [Gen 34:21 KJV]Only herein will the men consent unto us for to dwell with us, to be one people, if every male among us be circumcised, as they [are] circumcised. [Gen 34:22 KJV][Shall] not their cattle and their substance and every beast of theirs [be] ours? only let us consent unto them, and they will dwell with us. [Gen 34:23 KJV]And unto Hamor and unto Shechem his son hearkened all that went out of the gate of his city; and every male was circumcised, all that went out of the gate of his city. [Gen 34:24 KJV]And it came to pass on the third day, when they were sore, that two of the sons of Jacob, Simeon and Levi, Dinah's brethren, took each man his sword, and came upon the city boldly, and slew all the males. [Gen 34:25 KJV]And they slew Hamor and Shechem his son with the edge of the sword, and took Dinah out of Shechem's house, and went out. [Gen 34:26 KJV]The sons of Jacob came upon the slain, and spoiled the city, because they had defiled their sister. [Gen 34:27 KJV]They took their sheep, and their oxen, and their asses, and that which [was] in the city, and that which [was] in the field, [Gen 34:28 KJV]And all their wealth, and all their little ones, and their wives took they captive, and spoiled even all that [was] in the house. [Gen 34:29 KJV]And Jacob said to Simeon and Levi, Ye have troubled me to make me to stink among the inhabitants of the land, among the Canaanites and the Perizzites: and I [being] few in number, they shall gather themselves together against me, and slay me; and I shall be destroyed, I and my house. [Gen 34:30 KJV]And they said, Should he deal with our sister as with an harlot? [Gen 34:31 KJV]

CHAPTER 35

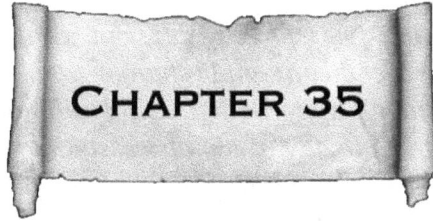

GOD SENDS JACOB TO BETHEL

God speaks to Jacob and tells him to go up to Bethel and dwell there and build an altar there where he was before when he was fleeing Esau. Then Jacob told his entire household to get rid of their strange gods, be clean, and change your clothes and they gave unto Jacob all the strange gods which were in their hand, and all their earrings which were in their ears; and Jacob hid them under the oak which was by Shechem. And they journeyed: and the terror of God was upon the cities that were round about them, and they did not pursue after the sons of Jacob.

The LORD kept His word to Jacob; He was with Him as He had promised. Jacob had thought that he and his family may be killed because of what his sons had done at Shechem. Immediately the LORD spoke to him and told him what to do and where to go. This must have eased his apprehension. He is beginning to understand that the LORD loves him just as He did his father Isaac and his grandfather Abraham. Situations and circumstances may change but the word of God never does.

When Jacob arrived at Bethel he built there an altar, and called the place Elbethel: because there God appeared unto him, when he fled from the face of his brother.

God appeared unto Jacob again, when he came out of Padanaram, and blessed him. And God said unto him:

- Thy name is Jacob: thy name shall not be called any more Jacob, but Israel shall be thy name: and he called his name Israel.
- And God said unto him, I am God Almighty: be fruitful and multiply
- A nation and a company of nations shall be of thee,
- and kings shall come out of thy loins;
- And the land which I gave Abraham and Isaac, to thee I will give it, and to thy seed after thee will I give the land.

And God went up from him in the place where he talked with him.

And God said unto Jacob, Arise, go up to Bethel, and dwell there: and make there an altar unto God, that appeared unto thee when thou fleddest from the face of Esau thy brother. [Gen 35:1 KJV] Then Jacob said unto his household, and to all that [were] with him, Put away the strange gods that [are] among you, and be clean, and change your garments: [Gen 35:2 KJV]And let us arise, and go up to Bethel; and I will make there an altar unto God, who answered me in the day of my distress, and was with me in the way which I went. [Gen 35:3 KJV]And they gave unto Jacob all the strange gods which [were] in their hand, and [all their] earrings which [were] in their ears; and Jacob hid them under the oak which [was] by Shechem. [Gen 35:4 KJV]And they journeyed: and the terror of God was upon the cities that [were] round about them, and they did not pursue after the sons of Jacob. [Gen 35:5 KJV]So Jacob came to Luz, which [is] in the land of Canaan, that [is], Bethel, he and all the people that [were] with him. [Gen 35:6 KJV]And he built there an altar, and called the place Elbethel: because there God appeared unto him, when he fled from the face of his brother. [Gen 35:7 KJV]But Deborah Rebekah's nurse died, and she was buried beneath Bethel under an oak: and the name of it was called Allonbachuth. [Gen 35:8 KJV]And God appeared unto Jacob again, when he came out of Padanaram, and blessed him. [Gen 35:9 KJV]And God said unto him, Thy name [is] Jacob: thy name shall not be called any more Jacob, but Israel shall be thy name: and he called his name Israel. [Gen 35:10 KJV]And God said unto him, I [am] God Almighty: be fruitful and multiply; a nation and a company of nations shall be of thee, and kings shall come out of thy loins; [Gen 35:11 KJV]And the land which I gave Abraham and Isaac, to thee I will give it, and to thy seed after thee will I give the land. [Gen 35:12 KJV]And God went up from him in the place where he talked with him. [Gen 35:13 KJV]And Jacob set up a pillar in the place where he talked with him, [even] a pillar of stone: and he poured a drink offering thereon, and he poured oil thereon. [Gen 35:14 KJV]And Jacob called the name of the place where God spake with him, Bethel. [Gen 35:15 KJV]

They traveled from Bethel on his way to Ephrath, and Rachael was in hard labor, the midwife told her that it was a boy and as her soul was departing she named him *'son of my sorrow'* - **Ben-oni** = son of my sorrow, but his father named him *'son of my right hand'* - **Benjamin** = son of the right hand. Rachael dies and was buried. And it came to pass, when Israel dwelt in that land, that **Reuben went and lay with Bilhah his father's concubine: and Israel heard it. Notice that Jacob is called Israel in this passage and he beginning to operate in his new name.**

And they journeyed from Bethel; and there was but a little way to come to Ephrath: and Rachel travailed, and she had hard labour. [Gen 35:16 KJV]And it came to pass, when she was in hard labour, that the midwife said unto her, Fear not; thou shalt have this son also. [Gen 35:17 KJV]And it came to pass, as her soul was in departing, (for she died) that she called his name

Benoni: but his father called him Benjamin. [Gen 35:18 KJV]And Rachel died, and was buried in the way to Ephrath, which [is] Bethlehem. [Gen 35:19 KJV]And Jacob set a pillar upon her grave: that [is] the pillar of Rachel's grave unto this day. [Gen 35:20 KJV]And Israel journeyed, and spread his tent beyond the tower of Edar. [Gen 35:21 KJV]And it came to pass, when Israel dwelt in that land, that Reuben went and lay with Bilhah his father's concubine: and Israel heard [it]. Now the sons of Jacob were twelve: [Gen 35:22 KJV]

Rachel is mentioned in the New Testament in Matthew 2:

In Rama was there a voice heard, lamentation, and weeping, and great mourning, Rachel weeping [for] her children, and would not be comforted, because they are not. [Mat 2:18 KJV]

This was because Herod had killed all the males two years old and younger.

Jacobs now has twelve sons and they are as follows:

The sons of Leah; Reuben, Jacob's firstborn, and Simeon, and Levi, and Judah, and Issachar, and Zebulun: [Gen 35:23 KJV]The sons of Rachel; Joseph, and Benjamin: [Gen 35:24 KJV]And the sons of Bilhah, Rachel's handmaid; Dan, and Naphtali: [Gen 35:25 KJV]And the sons of Zilpah, Leah's handmaid; Gad, and Asher: these [are] the sons of Jacob, which were born to him in Padanaram. [Gen 35:26 KJV]And Jacob came unto Isaac his father unto Mamre, unto the city of Arbah, which [is] Hebron, where Abraham and Isaac sojourned. [Gen 35:27 KJV]And the days of Isaac were an hundred and fourscore years. [Gen 35:28 KJV]And Isaac gave up the ghost, and died, and was gathered unto his people, [being] old and full of days: and his sons Esau and Jacob buried him. [Gen 35:29 KJV]

<u>God is awesome</u> – He knew **that Jacob must have twelve sons**, twelve is the number of government, but Jacob loved a woman that was not going to produce but two of them the woman that he did not love produced six of them and the two handmaidens produced the other four, this is amazing to me because it helps us understand that all things work for our good. God is good, and good cannot be defined without God, and God is love nor can love be defined without God. Jacob went through all that he did because God loved him, his family and all of us as well. Jacob did not seem to want any woman except Rachel and he did not seem interested in having multiple wives, in fact none of the extra wives were his choosing they were all given or suggested. Unlike Esau, who went after the extra wives, Jacob pursued only one.

CHAPTER 36

ESAU

Esau has so many cattle and people and property the space that he shared with his brother became too small so he left Canaan and dwelt in mount Seir. Esau is Edom, in this land the Esau produced dukes and kings before any kings reigned over the children of Israel. **As you follow the life of Esau in the New Testament you will come to know King Herod, who reigned during the time of Jesus and also to know that he was a descendant of Esau. He rebuilt the temple but it was for him because he wanted to please people and not to give God the glory. He wanted to please the Jews. The Romans considered him a king of the Jews and that is one of the possible reason he wanted the real king killed when he heard of his birth from the wise men who came to find him.**

You can also see the parallel with Cain and Esau the firstborn and the older brother did not want to follow God, they and their descendants rebelled against the God. They wanted to make natural history not spiritual history. Jacob like Able and Seth wanted to be connected with God and did not consider leaving God as an option, therefore in both cases the older brother had to serve the younger brother.

This is the biblical truth that God is trying to get to us from these types of relationships, the older brother serving the younger brother. The older brother 1st Adam is the brother of flesh, Jesus Christ the 2nd Adam is the younger brother of the spirit, the the flesh will always have to serve the spirit.

The following are the generations of Esau:

Now these [are] the generations of Esau, who [is] Edom. [Gen 36:1 KJV] Esau took his wives of the daughters of Canaan; Adah the daughter of Elon the Hittite, and Aholibamah the daughter of Anah the daughter of Zibeon the Hivite; [Gen 36:2 KJV]And Bashemath Ishmael's daughter, sister of Nebajoth. [Gen 36:3 KJV]And Adah bare to Esau Eliphaz; and Bashemath bare Reuel; [Gen 36:4 KJV]And Aholibamah bare Jeush, and Jaalam, and Korah: these [are] the sons of Esau, which were born unto him in the land of Canaan. [Gen 36:5 KJV]And Esau took his wives, and his sons, and his daughters, and all the persons of his house, and his cattle, and all his beasts, and all his substance, which he had got in the land of Canaan; and went into the country from the face of his brother Jacob. [Gen 36:6 KJV]For their riches were more than that they might dwell together; and the land wherein they were strangers could not bear them because of their cattle. [Gen 36:7 KJV]Thus dwelt Esau in mount Seir: Esau [is] Edom. [Gen 36:8 KJV]And these [are] the generations of Esau the father of the Edomites in mount Seir: [Gen 36:9 KJV]These [are] the names of Esau's sons; Eliphaz the son of Adah the wife of Esau, Reuel the son of Bashemath the wife of Esau. [Gen 36:10 KJV]And the sons of Eliphaz were Teman, Omar, Zepho, and Gatam, and Kenaz. [Gen 36:11 KJV]And Timna was concubine to Eliphaz Esau's son; and she bare to Eliphaz Amalek: these [were] the sons of Adah Esau's wife. [Gen 36:12 KJV]And these [are] the sons of Reuel; Nahath, and Zerah, Shammah, and Mizzah: these were the sons of Bashemath Esau's wife. [Gen 36:13 KJV]And these were the sons of Aholibamah, the daughter of Anah the daughter of Zibeon, Esau's wife: and she bare to Esau Jeush, and Jaalam, and Korah. [Gen 36:14 KJV]These [were] dukes of the sons of Esau: the sons of Eliphaz the firstborn [son] of Esau; duke Teman, duke Omar, duke Zepho, duke Kenaz, [Gen 36:15 KJV]Duke Korah, duke Gatam, [and] duke Amalek: these [are] the dukes [that came] of Eliphaz in the land of Edom; these [were] the sons of Adah. [Gen 36:16 KJV]And these [are] the sons of Reuel Esau's son; duke Nahath, duke Zerah, duke Shammah, duke Mizzah: these [are] the dukes [that came] of Reuel in the land of Edom; these [are] the sons of Bashemath Esau's wife. [Gen 36:17 KJV]And these [are] the sons of Aholibamah Esau's wife; duke Jeush, duke Jaalam, duke Korah: these [were] the dukes [that came] of Aholibamah the daughter of Anah, Esau's wife. [Gen 36:18 KJV]These [are] the sons of Esau, who [is] Edom, and these [are] their dukes. [Gen 36:19 KJV]These [are] the sons of Seir the Horite, who inhabited the land; Lotan, and Shobal, and Zibeon, and Anah, [Gen 36:20 KJV]And Dishon, and Ezer, and Dishan: these [are] the dukes of the Horites, the children of Seir in the land of Edom. [Gen 36:21 KJV]And the children of Lotan were Hori and Hemam; and Lotan's sister [was] Timna. [Gen 36:22 KJV]And the children of Shobal [were] these; Alvan, and Manahath, and Ebal, Shepho, and Onam. [Gen 36:23 KJV]And these [are] the children of Zibeon; both Ajah, and Anah: this [was that] Anah that found the mules in the wilderness, as he fed the asses of Zibeon his father. [Gen 36:24 KJV]And the children of Anah [were] these; Dishon, and Aholibamah the daughter of Anah. [Gen 36:25 KJV]And these [are] the children of Dishon; Hemdan, and Eshban, and Ithran, and Cheran. [Gen 36:26 KJV]The children of Ezer [are] these; Bilhan, and Zaavan, and Akan. [Gen 36:27 KJV]The children of Dishan [are] these; Uz, and Aran. [Gen 36:28 KJV]These [are] the dukes [that came] of the Horites; duke Lotan, duke Shobal, duke Zibeon, duke Anah, [Gen 36:29 KJV]Duke Dishon, duke Ezer, duke Dishan: these [are] the dukes [that came] of Hori, among their dukes in the land of Seir. [Gen 36:30 KJV] And these [are] the kings that reigned in the land of Edom, before there reigned any king over the children of Israel. [Gen 36:31 KJV]And Bela the son of Beor reigned in Edom: and the name of his city [was] Dinhabah. [Gen 36:32 KJV] And Bela died, and Jobab the son of Zerah of Bozrah reigned in his stead. [Gen 36:33 KJV]And Jobab died, and Husham of the land of Temani reigned in his stead. [Gen 36:34 KJV]And Husham died, and Hadad the son of Bedad, who smote Midian in the field of Moab, reigned in his stead: and the name of his city [was] Avith. [Gen 36:35 KJV]And Hadad died, and Samlah of Masrekah reigned in his stead. [Gen 36:36 KJV]And Samlah died, and Saul of Rehoboth [by] the river reigned in his stead. [Gen 36:37 KJV]And Saul died, and Baalhanan the son of Achbor reigned in his stead. [Gen 36:38 KJV]And Baalhanan the son of Achbor died, and Hadar reigned in his stead: and the name of his city [was] Pau; and his wife's name [was] Mehetabel, the daughter of Matred, the daughter of Mezahab. [Gen 36:39 KJV]

CHAPTER 37

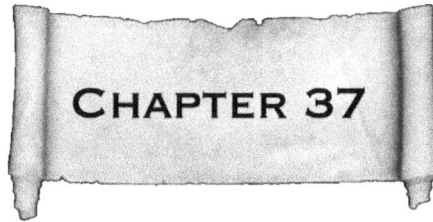

JOSEPH SOLD BY HIS BROTHERS

THE LIFE OF JOSEPH CHAPTERS 37-50

Jacob loved Joseph more than all of his children because he was the son of his old age and he made him a coat of many colors and when his brothers saw that their father loved him more they hated him and could not speak peaceable to him. Joseph was a dreamer and he had a dream (For, behold, we were binding sheaves in the field, and, lo, my sheaf arose, and also stood upright; and, behold, your sheaves stood round about, and made obeisance to my sheaf.) and his brothers hated him even the more for his dream and for his words.

And he dreamed yet another dream, and told it his brethren, and said, Behold, I have dreamed a dream more; and, behold, the sun and the moon and the eleven stars made obeisance to me. And he told it to his father, and to his brethren: and his father rebuked him, and said unto him, what is this dream that thou hast dreamed? Shall I and thy mother and thy brethren indeed come to bow down ourselves to thee to the earth? And his brethren envied him; but his father observed the saying.

Jacob sent Joseph to check on his brothers that were feeding the flocks in fields away from home, **when they saw him they decided to kill him but Reuben convinced them not to kill him but to put him in a dry well. Reuben intended to take him back to Jacob but while they were eating bread they looked up and saw Ishmaelites traders and Judah came up with the idea to sell him to the Ishmaelites. They reasoned let not our hand be upon him; for he is our brother and our flesh.** And his brethren were content. In the meantime some **Midianite** passed by, they pulled him up and lifted Joseph out of the pit, and sold him to the **Ishmaelites** for twenty shekels of silver. Thus they brought Joseph into Egypt.

Joseph passed through the hands of the Ishmaelites and the Midianites both of which were sons of Abraham via Hagar and Keturah.

Who were the Ishmaelites?

Ishmael, son of Abraham and Hagar. [Gen 25:13–15]

The Ishmaelites are the decedents of Ishmael, the son of Abraham and Hagar.

Who were the Midianites?

According to Genesis 25, the Midianites were the descendants of Midian, who was a son of Abraham through his wife Keturah:

". . . again Abraham took a wife, and her name was Keturah. And she bare him Zimran, and Jokshan, and Medan, and Midian, and Ishbak, and Shuah." [Gens 25:1-2, KJV]

Joseph's brothers took Joseph's coat, and killed a kid of the goats, and dipped the coat in the blood then they brought the coat of many colors to their father; and said that they had found it and pretended that they did not know it was Joseph's coat, but Jacob said it is my son's coat an evil beast hath devoured him.

Jacob rent his clothes, and put sackcloth upon his loins, and mourned for his son many days. And all his sons and all his daughters rose up to comfort him; but he refused to be comforted; and he said, I will go down into the grave unto my son mourning. Thus his father wept for him.

And Jacob dwelt in the land wherein his father was a stranger, in the land of Canaan. [Gen 37:1 KJV]These [are] the generations of Jacob. Joseph, [being] seventeen years old, was feeding the flock with his brethren; and the lad [was] with the sons of Bilhah, and with the sons of Zilpah, his father's wives: and Joseph brought unto his father their evil report. [Gen 37:2 KJV]Now Israel loved Joseph more than all his children, because he [was] the son of his old age: and he made him a coat of [many] colours. [Gen 37:3 KJV]And when his brethren saw that their father loved him more than all his brethren, they hated him, and could not speak peaceably unto him. [Gen 37:4 KJV]And Joseph dreamed a dream, and he told [it] his brethren: and they hated him yet the more. [Gen 37:5 KJV]And he said unto them, Hear, I pray you, this dream which I have dreamed: [Gen 37:6 KJVFor, behold, we [were] binding sheaves in the field, and, lo, my sheaf arose, and also stood upright; and, behold, your sheaves stood round about, and made obeisance to my sheaf. [Gen 37:7 KJV]And his brethren said to him, Shalt thou indeed reign over us? or shalt thou indeed have dominion over us? And they hated him yet the more for his dreams, and for his words. [Gen 37:8 KJV]And he dreamed yet another dream, and told it his brethren, and said, Behold, I have dreamed a dream more; and, behold, the sun and the moon and the eleven stars made obeisance to me. [Gen 37:9 KJV]And he told [it] to his father, and to his brethren: and his father rebuked him, and said unto him, What [is] this dream that thou hast dreamed? Shall I and thy mother and thy brethren indeed come to bow down ourselves to thee to the earth? [Gen 37:10 KJV]And his brethren envied him; but his father observed the saying. [Gen 37:11 KJV]And his brethren went to feed their father's flock in Shechem. [Gen 37:12 KJV]And Israel said unto Joseph, Do not thy brethren feed [the flock] in Shechem? come, and I will send thee unto them. And he said to him, Here [am I]. [Gen 37:13 KJV]And he said to him, Go, I pray thee, see whether it be well with thy brethren, and well with the flocks; and bring me word again. So he sent him out of the vale of Hebron, and he came to Shechem. [Gen 37:14 KJV]And a certain man found him, and, behold, [he was] wandering in the field: and the man asked him, saying, What seekest thou? [Gen 37:15 KJV]And he said, I seek my brethren: tell me, I pray thee, where they feed [their flocks]. [Gen 37:16 KJV]And the man said, They are departed hence; for I heard them say, Let us go to Dothan. And Joseph went after his brethren, and found them in Dothan. [Gen 37:17 KJV]And when they saw him afar off, even before he came near unto them, they conspired against him to slay him. [Gen 37:18 KJV]And they said one to another, Behold, this dreamer cometh. [Gen 37:19 KJV]Come now therefore, and let us slay him, and cast him into some pit, and we will say, Some evil beast hath devoured him: and we shall see what will become of his dreams. [Gen 37:20 KJV]And Reuben heard [it], and he delivered him out of their hands; and said, Let us not kill him. [Gen 37:21 KJV] And Reuben said unto them, Shed no blood, [but] cast him into this pit that [is] in the wilderness, and lay no hand upon him; that he might rid him out of their hands, to deliver him to his father again. [Gen 37:22 KJV]And it came to pass, when Joseph was come unto his brethren, that they stript Joseph out of his coat, [his] coat of [many] colours that [was] on him; [Gen 37:23 KJV]And they took him, and cast him into a pit: and the pit [was] empty, [there was] no water in it. [Gen 37:24 KJV]And they sat down to eat bread: and they lifted up their eyes and looked, and, behold, a company of Ishmaelites came from Gilead with their camels bearing spicery and balm and myrrh, going to carry [it] down to Egypt. [Gen 37:25 KJV]And Judah said unto his brethren, What profit [is it] if we slay our brother, and conceal his blood? [Gen 37:26 KJV]Come, and let us sell him to the Ishmaelites, and let not our hand be upon him; for he [is] our brother [and] our flesh. And his brethren were content. [Gen 37:27 KJV]Then there passed by Midianites merchantmen; and they drew and lifted up Joseph out of the pit, and sold Joseph to the Ishmaelites for twenty [pieces] of silver: and they brought Joseph into Egypt. [Gen 37:28 KJV]And Reuben returned unto the pit; and, behold, Joseph [was] not in the pit; and he rent his clothes. [Gen 37:29 KJV]And he returned unto his brethren, and said, The child [is] not; and I, whither shall I go? [Gen 37:30 KJV]And they took Joseph's coat, and killed a kid of the goats, and dipped the coat in the blood; [Gen 37:31 KJV]And they sent the coat of [many] colours, and they brought [it] to their father; and said, This have we found: know now whether it [be] thy son's coat or no. [Gen 37:32 KJV]And he knew it, and said, [It is] my son's coat; an evil beast hath devoured him; Joseph is without doubt rent in pieces. [Gen 37:33 KJV]And Jacob rent his clothes, and put sackcloth upon his loins, and mourned for his son many days. [Gen 37:34 KJV] And all his sons and all his daughters rose up to comfort him; but he refused to be comforted; and he said, For I will go down into the grave unto my son mourning. Thus his father wept for him. [Gen 37:35 KJV]And the Midianites sold him into Egypt unto Potiphar, an officer of Pharaoh's, [and] captain of the guard. [Gen 37:36 KJV]

CHAPTER 38

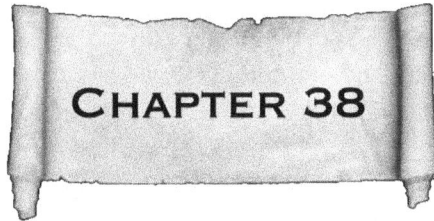

JUDAH AND TAMAR

It is interesting to me that the subject would now switch to Judah, since he was the one who came up with the idea to sell his brother.

Judah went to visit a friend Hirah and while there he met a Canaanite woman named Shuah and he had three sons by her Er, Onan and Shelah. Judah took a wife for Er whose name was Tamar. Er was wicked before the LORD so the LORD slew him. Then Judah told Onan to go into his brother's wife and marry her and raise up seed to his brother but when he went in to her he spilled the seed onto the ground because he did not want her to have what belonged to him and his seed. Therefore, God killed him also.

Then Judah said to Tamar his daughter in law, remain a widow at thy father's house, till Shelah my son be grown: for he said, Lest he die also, as his brethren did. And Tamar went and dwelt in her father's house. Judah's wife died and after that happened some time later he went with his friend to sheep shearers and Tamar was told of it, she took off her widow clothing and covered herself with a veil for she saw that Shelah was grown, and she was not given unto him to wife.

When Judah saw her, he thought she was a harlot; because she had covered her face. And he turned unto her by the way, and said, let me come in unto you; he did not know that she was his daughter-in-law. She asked what he will give her, if I say yes. And he said, I will send you a kid from the flock. Then she said, will you give me something as a pledge to send it? And he said, what pledge shall I give you? And she said, your signet, and your bracelets, and your staff that's in your hand, he gave them to her, and came in unto her, and she conceived by him.

When Judah tried to send her the kid by his friend to collect his pledge the woman could not be found and the men of the city said that there is not harlot in this city.

Later Judah heard that Tamar was with child. It had been three months since Judah had his encounter with Tamar. Someone came to him and said Tamar your daughter in law hath played the harlot; and also, behold, she is with child by whoredom. And Judah said, bring her forth, and let her be burnt. When she was brought forth, she sent to her father in law, saying, the man, whose these are, am I with child: and she said, whose are these, the signet, and bracelets, and staff. Then Judah acknowledged them and said, She hath been more righteous than I; because I gave her not to Shelah my son. And he knew her again no more. And it came to pass in the time of her travail that, behold, twins in her womb. **And it came to pass, when she travailed, that the one put out his hand: and the midwife took and bound upon his hand a scarlet thread, saying, This one came out first. And it came to pass, as he drew back his hand, and then behold, his brother came out: and she said, how hast thou broken forth? Breach upon thee: therefore his name was called Pharez. And afterward came out his brother, who had the scarlet thread upon his hand: and his name was called Zarah.**

Pharez switched positions in the womb, he was in fact the youngest but he over powered his brother and is now born first, and even in this case the older will serve the younger.

Who is Pharez? He was ancestor of … Boaz, Obed, Jesse and King David.

And it came to pass at that time, that Judah went down from his brethren, and turned in to a certain Adullamite, whose name [was] Hirah. [Gen 38:1 KJV] And Judah saw there a daughter of a certain Canaanite, whose name [was] Shuah; and he took her, and went in unto her. [Gen 38:2 KJV]And she conceived, and bare a son; and he called his name Er. [Gen 38:3 KJV]And she conceived again, and bare a son; and she called his name Onan. [Gen 38:4 KJV]And she yet again conceived, and bare a son; and called his name Shelah: and he was at Chezib, when she bare him. [Gen 38:5 KJV]And Judah took a wife for Er his firstborn, whose name [was] Tamar. [Gen 38:6 KJV]And Er, Judah's firstborn, was wicked in the sight of the LORD; and the LORD slew him. [Gen 38:7 KJV]And Judah said unto Onan, Go in unto thy brother's wife, and marry her, and raise up seed to thy brother. [Gen 38:8 KJV]And Onan knew that the seed should not be his; and it came to pass, when he went in unto his brother's wife, that he spilled [it] on the ground, lest that he should give seed to his brother. [Gen 38:9 KJV]And the thing which he did displeased the LORD: wherefore he slew him also. [Gen 38:10 KJV]Then said Judah to Tamar his daughter in law, Remain a widow at thy father's house, till Shelah my son be grown: for he said, Lest peradventure he die also, as his brethren [did]. And Tamar went and dwelt in her father's house. [Gen 38:11 KJV]And in process of time the daughter of Shuah Judah's wife died; and Judah was comforted, and went up unto his sheepshearers to Timnath, he and his friend Hirah the Adullamite. [Gen 38:12 KJV]And it was told Tamar, saying, Behold thy father in law goeth up to Timnath to shear his sheep. [Gen 38:13 KJV]And she put her widow's garments off from her, and covered her with a vail, and wrapped herself, and sat in an open place, which [is] by the way to Timnath;

for she saw that Shelah was grown, and she was not given unto him to wife. [Gen 38:14 KJV]When Judah saw her, he thought her [to be] an harlot; because she had covered her face. [Gen 38:15 KJV]And he turned unto her by the way, and said, Go to, I pray thee, let me come in unto thee; (for he knew not that she [was] his daughter in law.) And she said, What wilt thou give me, that thou mayest come in unto me? [Gen 38:16 KJV]And he said, I will send [thee] a kid from the flock. And she said, Wilt thou give [me] a pledge, till thou send [it]? [Gen 38:17 KJV]And he said, What pledge shall I give thee? And she said, Thy signet, and thy bracelets, and thy staff that [is] in thine hand. And he gave [it] her, and came in unto her, and she conceived by him. [Gen 38:18 KJV]And she arose, and went away, and laid by her vail from her, and put on the garments of her widowhood. [Gen 38:19 KJV]And Judah sent the kid by the hand of his friend the Adullamite, to receive [his] pledge from the woman's hand: but he found her not. [Gen 38:20 KJV]Then he asked the men of that place, saying, Where [is] the harlot, that [was] openly by the way side? And they said, There was no harlot in this [place]. [Gen 38:21 KJV]And he returned to Judah, and said, I cannot find her; and also the men of the place said, [that] there was no harlot in this [place]. [Gen 38:22 KJV]And Judah said, Let her take [it] to her, lest we be shamed: behold, I sent this kid, and thou hast not found her. [Gen 38:23 KJV]And it came to pass about three months after, that it was told Judah, saying, Tamar thy daughter in law hath played the harlot; and also, behold, she [is] with child by whoredom. And Judah said, Bring her forth, and let her be burnt. [Gen 38:24 KJV]When she [was] brought forth, she sent to her father in law, saying, By the man, whose these [are, am] I with child: and she said, Discern, I pray thee, whose [are] these, the signet, and bracelets, and staff. [Gen 38:25 KJV]And Judah acknowledged [them], and said, She hath been more righteous than I; because that I gave her not to Shelah my son. And he knew her again no more. [Gen 38:26 KJV]And it came to pass in the time of her travail, that, behold, twins [were] in her womb. [Gen 38:27 KJV]And it came to pass, when she travailed, that [the one] put out [his] hand: and the midwife took and bound upon his hand a scarlet thread, saying, This came out first. [Gen 38:28 KJV]And it came to pass, as he drew back his hand, that, behold, his brother came out: and she said, How hast thou broken forth? [this] breach [be] upon thee: therefore his name was called Pharez. [Gen 38:29 KJV]And afterward came out his brother, that had the scarlet thread upon his hand: and his name was called Zarah. [Gen 38:30 KJV]

CHAPTER 39

JOSEPH TAKEN TO EGYPT AND IMPRISONED

How was Joseph going to get to Egypt, God had mentioned to Abraham that his seed shall be a stranger in a land that is not theirs and shall be afflicted four hundred years. God was taking to Abraham but he never mentioned Egypt. Jacob knew that he could not leave the land that he was living on at that time until God told him to leave. Since God had not given him direction to go to Egypt he would have never gone, nor would it ever occurred to him to send Joseph anywhere not to mention that far away. However, Joseph must eventually end up in Egypt.

This is an amazing story, can you imagine how God must have comforted Joseph during this process of transition. He was considered the most favored in his family dynamics and now he finds himself a slave in a strange land with what appears to be no possibility of ever seeing his family again. What an opportunity to become bitter, angry, and to give up or quit, but with the help of the LORD he made it through the process.

Joseph was sold to Potiphar, an Egyptian, an officer of Pharaoh, captain of the guard. Joseph was an excellent manager. God was with him and he was prosperous. When Potiphar saw that the LORD was with him and everything that he put his hands to prospered he made him overseer over his house and all that he had and the LORD prospered Potiphar for Joseph's sake.

Potiphar's wife tried to seduce Joseph and when Joseph resisted she lied on him and said that he attacked her. As a result Joseph's master took him, and put him into the prison, a place where the king's prisoners were kept and he was there in the prison with them. But the LORD was with Joseph, and shewed him mercy, and gave him favor in the sight of the keeper of the prison.

And Joseph was brought down to Egypt; and Potiphar, an officer of Pharaoh, captain of the guard, an Egyptian, bought him of the hands of the Ishmaelites, which had brought him down thither. [Gen 39:1 KJV] And the LORD was with Joseph, and he was a prosperous man; and he was in the house of his master the Egyptian. [Gen 39:2 KJV]And his master saw that the LORD [was] with him, and that the LORD made all that he did to prosper in his hand. [Gen 39:3 KJV] And Joseph found grace in his sight, and he served him: and he

*made him overseer over his house, and all [that] he had he put into his hand.
[Gen 39:4 KJV]And it came to pass from the time [that] he had made him
overseer in his house, and over all that he had, that the LORD blessed the
Egyptian's house for Joseph's sake; and the blessing of the LORD was upon
all that he had in the house, and in the field. [Gen 39:5 KJV]And he left all
that he had in Joseph's hand; and he knew not ought he had, save the bread
which he did eat. And Joseph was [a] goodly [person], and well favoured.
[Gen 39:6 KJV]And it came to pass after these things, that his master's wife
cast her eyes upon Joseph; and she said, Lie with me. [Gen 39:7 KJV]But he
refused, and said unto his master's wife, Behold, my master wotteth not what
[is] with me in the house, and he hath committed all that he hath to my hand;
[Gen 39:8 KJV][There is] none greater in this house than I; neither hath he
kept back any thing from me but thee, because thou [art] his wife: how then
can I do this great wickedness, and sin against God? [Gen 39:9 KJV]And it
came to pass, as she spake to Joseph day by day, that he hearkened not unto
her, to lie by her, [or] to be with her. [Gen 39:10 KJV]And it came to pass
about this time, that [Joseph] went into the house to do his business; and
[there was] none of the men of the house there within. [Gen 39:11 KJV]And
she caught him by his garment, saying, Lie with me: and he left his garment
in her hand, and fled, and got him out. [Gen 39:12 KJV]And it came to pass,
when she saw that he had left his garment in her hand, and was fled forth,
[Gen 39:13 KJV]That she called unto the men of her house, and spake unto
them, saying, See, he hath brought in an Hebrew unto us to mock us; he came
in unto me to lie with me, and I cried with a loud voice: [Gen 39:14 KJV]And
it came to pass, when he heard that I lifted up my voice and cried, that he left
his garment with me, and fled, and got him out. [Gen 39:15 KJV] And she laid
up his garment by her, until his lord came home. [Gen 39:16 KJV] And she
spake unto him according to these words, saying, The Hebrew servant, which
thou hast brought unto us, came in unto me to mock me: [Gen 39:17
KJV]And it came to pass, as I lifted up my voice and cried, that he left his
garment with me, and fled out. [Gen 39:18 KJV]And it came to pass, when his
master heard the words of his wife, which she spake unto him, saying, After
this manner did thy servant to me; that his wrath was kindled. [Gen 39:19
KJV]And Joseph's master took him, and put him into the prison, a place
where the king's prisoners [were] bound: and he was there in the prison. [Gen
39:20 KJV]But the LORD was with Joseph, and shewed him mercy, and gave
him favour in the sight of the keeper of the prison. [Gen 39:21 KJV]And the
keeper of the prison committed to Joseph's hand all the prisoners that [were]
in the prison; and whatsoever they did there, he was the doer [of it]. [Gen
39:22 KJV]The keeper of the prison looked not to any thing [that was] under
his hand; because the LORD was with him, and [that] which he did, the
LORD made [it] to prosper. [Gen 39:23 KJV]*

CHAPTER 40

JOSEPH IN PRISON

After a time the butler of the king of Egypt and his baker offended their king and he had them put in prison. While they were there they both had dreams that Joseph was able to interpret. The interpretations that Joseph gave were accurate and each one did come to pass. The baker was told that the king would behead him; the butler was told that the king would restore him. Joseph asked the butler to remember him when he returned to the king because he had done nothing to be in prison, but the butler did not remember him when he returned.

And it came to pass after these things, [that] the butler of the king of Egypt and [his] baker had offended their lord the king of Egypt. [Gen 40:1 KJV]And Pharaoh was wroth against two [of] his officers, against the chief of the butlers, and against the chief of the bakers. [Gen 40:2 KJV]And he put them in ward in the house of the captain of the guard, into the prison, the place where Joseph [was] bound. [Gen 40:3 KJV]And the captain of the guard charged Joseph with them, and he served them: and they continued a season in ward. [Gen 40:4 KJV]And they dreamed a dream both of them, each man his dream in one night, each man according to the interpretation of his dream, the butler and the baker of the king of Egypt, which [were] bound in the prison. [Gen 40:5 KJV]And Joseph came in unto them in the morning, and looked upon them, and, behold, they [were] sad. [Gen 40:6 KJV]And he asked Pharaoh's officers that [were] with him in the ward of his lord's house, saying, Wherefore look ye [so] sadly to day? [Gen 40:7 KJV]And they said unto him, We have dreamed a dream, and [there is] no interpreter of it. And Joseph said unto them, [Do] not interpretations [belong] to God? tell me [them], I pray you. [Gen 40:8 KJV]And the chief butler told his dream to Joseph, and said to him, In my dream, behold, a vine [was] before me; [Gen 40:9 KJV]And in the vine [were] three branches: and it [was] as though it budded, [and] her blossoms shot forth; and the clusters thereof brought forth ripe grapes: [Gen 40:10 KJV]And Pharaoh's cup [was] in my hand: and I took the grapes, and pressed them into Pharaoh's cup, and I gave the cup into Pharaoh's hand. [Gen 40:11 KJV]And Joseph said unto him, This [is] the interpretation of it: The three branches [are] three days: [Gen 40:12 KJV]Yet within three days shall Pharaoh lift up thine head, and restore thee unto thy place: and thou shalt deliver Pharaoh's cup into his hand, after the former manner when thou wast his butler. [Gen 40:13 KJV]But think on me when it shall be well with thee, and shew kindness, I pray thee, unto me, and make mention of me unto Pharaoh, and bring me out of this house: [Gen 40:14 KJV]For indeed I was stolen away out of the land of the Hebrews: and here also have I done nothing that they should put me into the dungeon. [Gen 40:15 KJV] When the chief baker saw that the interpretation was good, he said unto Joseph, I also [was] in my dream, and, behold, [I had] three white baskets on my head: [Gen 40:16 KJV]And in the uppermost basket [there was] of all manner of bakemeats for Pharaoh; and the birds did eat them out of the basket upon my head. [Gen 40:17 KJV]And Joseph answered and said, This [is] the interpretation thereof: The three baskets [are] three days: [Gen 40:18 KJV] Yet within three days shall Pharaoh lift up thy head from off thee, and shall hang thee on a tree; and the birds shall eat thy flesh from off thee. [Gen 40:19 KJV]And it came to pass the third day, [which was] Pharaoh's birthday, that he made a feast unto all his servants: and he lifted up the head of the chief butler and of the chief baker among his servants. [Gen 40:20 KJV]And he restored the chief butler unto his butlership again; and he gave the cup into Pharaoh's hand: [Gen 40:21 KJV]But he hanged the chief baker: as Joseph had interpreted to them. [Gen 40:22 KJV]Yet did not the chief butler remember Joseph, but forgat him. [Gen 40:23 KJV]

CHAPTER 41

JOSEPH RELEASED FROM PRISON

After Joseph spent two years in prison, Pharaoh had a dream that troubled him and he called for all the magicians of Egypt and all the wise men and he told them his dream; but there was none that could interpret them unto Pharaoh.

The butler remembered Joseph and told Pharaoh of Joseph's ability to interpret dreams accurately. Pharaoh sent for Joseph to interpret his dreams. Joseph was able to interpret the dreams. Joseph told Pharaoh the interpretations, however, Joseph did let Pharaoh know that it was the LORD that had given him the interpretation of dreams. Joseph told Pharaoh God hath showed Pharaoh what He is about to do and there would be seven years of plenty and seven years of famine, and then he suggested what Pharaoh should do to successfully survive the famine. Pharaoh decided to put Joseph in charge of the survival plan that Joseph suggested that Pharaoh put in place. **Pharaoh asked of his servants can we find such a one as this, a man in whom the Spirit of God is. Pharaoh's servants agreed, then Pharaoh said unto Joseph, Forasmuch as God hath shewed thee all this, there is none so discreet and wise as you are, you shalt be over my house, and according unto thy word shall all my people be ruled: only in the throne will I be greater than you. Pharaoh said unto Joseph, See, I have set thee over all the land of Egypt. And Pharaoh took off his ring from his hand, and put it upon Joseph's hand, and arrayed him in vestures of fine linen, and put a gold chain about his neck; And he made him to ride in the second chariot which he had; and they cried before him, Bow the knee: and he made him ruler over all the land of Egypt. Pharaoh said unto Joseph, I am Pharaoh, and without thee shall no man lift up his hand or foot in all the land of Egypt.** Pharaoh called Joseph's name Zaphnathpaaneah; and he gave him to wife Asenath the daughter of Potipherah priest of On. And Joseph went out over all the land of Egypt. And Joseph was thirty years old when he stood before Pharaoh king of Egypt. And Joseph went out from the presence of Pharaoh, and went throughout all the land of Egypt.

Joseph stored a fifth of all the corn that was harvested in the seven plenteous years the earth brought forth by handfuls. Joseph gathered up all the food of the seven years, which were in the land of Egypt, and laid up the food in the cities: the food of the field, which was round about every city, did the same. And Joseph gathered corn as the sand of the sea, very much, until he left numbering;

for it was without number.

And it came to pass at the end of two full years, that Pharaoh dreamed: and, behold, he stood by the river. [Gen 41:1 KJV]And, behold, there came up out of the river seven well favoured kine and fatfleshed; and they fed in a meadow. [Gen 41:2 KJV]And, behold, seven other kine came up after them out of the river, ill favoured and leanfleshed; and stood by the [other] kine upon the brink of the river. [Gen 41:3 KJV]And the ill favoured and leanfleshed kine did eat up the seven well favoured and fat kine. So Pharaoh awoke. [Gen 41:4 KJV]And he slept and dreamed the second time: and, behold, seven ears of corn came up upon one stalk, rank and good. [Gen 41:5 KJV]And, behold, seven thin ears and blasted with the east wind sprung up after them. [Gen 41:6 KJV]And the seven thin ears devoured the seven rank and full ears. And Pharaoh awoke, and, behold, [it was] a dream. [Gen 41:7 KJV]And it came to pass in the morning that his spirit was troubled; and he sent and called for all the magicians of Egypt, and all the wise men thereof: and Pharaoh told them his dream; but [there was] none that could interpret them unto Pharaoh. [Gen 41:8 KJV]Then spake the chief butler unto Pharaoh, saying, I do remember my faults this day: [Gen 41:9 KJV]Pharaoh was wroth with his servants, and put me in ward in the captain of the guard's house, [both] me and the chief baker: [Gen 41:10 KJV]And we dreamed a dream in one night, I and he; we dreamed each man according to the interpretation of his dream. [Gen 41:11 KJV]And [there was] there with us a young man, an Hebrew, servant to the captain of the guard; and we told him, and he interpreted to us our dreams; to each man according to his dream he did interpret. [Gen 41:12 KJV]And it came to pass, as he interpreted to us, so it was; me he restored unto mine office, and him he hanged. [Gen 41:13 KJV]Then Pharaoh sent and called Joseph, and they brought him hastily out of the dungeon: and he shaved [himself], and changed his raiment, and came in unto Pharaoh. [Gen 41:14 KJV]And Pharaoh said unto Joseph, I have dreamed a dream, and [there is] none that can interpret it: and I have heard say of thee, [that] thou canst understand a dream to interpret it. [Gen 41:15 KJV] And Joseph answered Pharaoh, saying, [It is] not in me: God shall give Pharaoh an answer of peace. [Gen 41:16 KJV]And Pharaoh said unto Joseph, In my dream, behold, I stood upon the bank of the river: [Gen 41:17 KJV]And, behold, there came up out of the river seven kine, fatfleshed and well favoured; and they fed in a meadow: [Gen 41:18 KJV]And, behold, seven other kine came up after them, poor and very ill favoured and leanfleshed, such as I never saw in all the land of Egypt for badness: [Gen 41:19 KJV]And the lean and the ill favoured kine did eat up the first seven fat kine: [Gen 41:20 KJV]And when they had eaten them up, it could not be known that they had eaten them; but they [were] still ill favoured, as at the beginning. So I awoke. [Gen 41:21 KJV] And I saw in my dream, and, behold, seven ears came up in one stalk, full and good: [Gen

41:22 KJV]And, behold, seven ears, withered, thin, [and] blasted with the east wind, sprung up after them: [Gen 41:23 KJV]And the thin ears devoured the seven good ears: and I told [this] unto the magicians; but [there was] none that could declare [it] to me. [Gen 41:24 KJV]And Joseph said unto Pharaoh, The dream of Pharaoh [is] one: God hath shewed Pharaoh what he [is] about to do. [Gen 41:25 KJV]The seven good kine [are] seven years; and the seven good ears [are] seven years: the dream [is] one. [Gen 41:26 KJV]And the seven thin and ill favoured kine that came up after them [are] seven years; and the seven empty ears blasted with the east wind shall be seven years of famine. [Gen 41:27 KJV]This [is] the thing which I have spoken unto Pharaoh: What God [is] about to do he sheweth unto Pharaoh. [Gen 41:28 KJV]Behold, there come seven years of great plenty throughout all the land of Egypt: [Gen 41:29 KJV]And there shall arise after them seven years of famine; and all the plenty shall be forgotten in the land of Egypt; and the famine shall consume the land; [Gen 41:30 KJV]And the plenty shall not be known in the land by reason of that famine following; for it [shall be] very grievous. [Gen 41:31 KJV]And for that the dream was doubled unto Pharaoh twice; [it is] because the thing [is] established by God, and God will shortly bring it to pass. [Gen 41:32 KJV]Now therefore let Pharaoh look out a man discreet and wise, and set him over the land of Egypt. [Gen 41:33 KJV]Let Pharaoh do [this], and let him appoint officers over the land, and take up the fifth part of the land of Egypt in the seven plenteous years. [Gen 41:34 KJV]And let them gather all the food of those good years that come, and lay up corn under the hand of Pharaoh, and let them keep food in the cities. [Gen 41:35 KJV]And that food shall be for store to the land against the seven years of famine, which shall be in the land of Egypt; that the land perish not through the famine. [Gen 41:36 KJV]And the thing was good in the eyes of Pharaoh, and in the eyes of all his servants. [Gen 41:37 KJV]And Pharaoh said unto his servants, Can we find [such a one] as this [is], a man in whom the Spirit of God [is]? [Gen 41:38 KJV]And Pharaoh said unto Joseph, Forasmuch as God hath shewed thee all this, [there is] none so discreet and wise as thou [art]: [Gen 41:39 KJV]Thou shalt be over my house, and according unto thy word shall all my people be ruled: only in the throne will I be greater than thou. [Gen 41:40 KJV]And Pharaoh said unto Joseph, See, I have set thee over all the land of Egypt. [Gen 41:41 KJV]And Pharaoh took off his ring from his hand, and put it upon Joseph's hand, and arrayed him in vestures of fine linen, and put a gold chain about his neck; [Gen 41:42 KJV]And he made him to ride in the second chariot which he had; and they cried before him, Bow the knee: and he made him [ruler] over all the land of Egypt. [Gen 41:43 KJV] And Pharaoh said unto Joseph, I [am] Pharaoh, and without thee shall no man lift up his hand or foot in all the land of Egypt. [Gen 41:44 KJV]And Pharaoh called Joseph's name Zaphnathpaaneah; and he gave him to wife Asenath the daughter of Potipherah priest of On. And

Joseph went out over [all] the land of Egypt. [Gen 41:45 KJV]And Joseph [was] thirty years old when he stood before Pharaoh king of Egypt. And Joseph went out from the presence of Pharaoh, and went throughout all the land of Egypt. [Gen 41:46 KJV]And in the seven plenteous years the earth brought forth by handfuls. [Gen 41:47 KJV]And he gathered up all the food of the seven years, which were in the land of Egypt, and laid up the food in the cities: the food of the field, which [was] round about every city, laid he up in the same. [Gen 41:48 KJV]And Joseph gathered corn as the sand of the sea, very much, until he left numbering; for [it was] without number. [Gen 41:49 KJV]

Joseph had two sons born to him before the famine; he named the first born son 'causing to forget', Manasseh = causing to forget for he said the LORD has made me forget all my toil and all my father's house and he named his second son Ephraim = 'double ash-heap': I shall be doubly fruitful" and Joseph said God hath caused me to be fruitful in the land of my affliction.

And unto Joseph were born two sons before the years of famine came, which Asenath the daughter of Potipherah priest of On bare unto him. [Gen 41:50 KJV]And Joseph called the name of the firstborn Manasseh: For God, [said he], hath made me forget all my toil, and all my father's house. [Gen 41:51 KJV]And the name of the second called he Ephraim: For God hath caused me to be fruitful in the land of my affliction. [Gen 41:52 KJV]And the seven years of plenteousness, that was in the land of Egypt, were ended. [Gen 41:53 KJV]And the seven years of dearth began to come, according as Joseph had said: and the dearth was in all lands; but in all the land of Egypt there was bread. [Gen 41:54 KJV]And when all the land of Egypt was famished, the people cried to Pharaoh for bread: and Pharaoh said unto all the Egyptians, Go unto Joseph; what he saith to you, do. [Gen 41:55 KJV]And the famine was over all the face of the earth: And Joseph opened all the storehouses, and sold unto the Egyptians; and the famine waxed sore in the land of Egypt. [Gen 41:56 KJV]And all countries came into Egypt to Joseph for to buy [corn]; because that the famine was [so] sore in all lands. [Gen 41:57 KJV]

Notice that Joseph received double of his father's inheritance.

CHAPTER 42-44

JOSEPH REUNITES WITH HIS BROTHERS

There was famine in the land and Egypt was the only place where there was food. When Jacob saw that there was corn in Egypt he sent his ten sons to go down to Egypt and get food. They did not take Benjamin because Jacob would not let him go for fear of something happening to him.

When Joseph saw them he recognized them but they did not recognize him. He spoke harshly to them Joseph's brethren came, and bowed down themselves before him with their faces to the earth.

Joseph remembered his dream, then he accused them of being spies, they said that they were not spies but the sons of one man. Joseph accused them of being spies again and they said, we are twelve brothers and are the sons of one man in the land of Canaan. Our youngest brother is home with our father, and one is not. Joseph asked them to prove that they were not spies by bringing their younger brother to him. Then he said send one of you and let him fetch your brother, and you shall be kept in prison, that your words may be proved, whether there be any truth in you: or else by the life of Pharaoh surely you are spies. Rueben spoke to his brothers reminding them that he had told them not to sin against Joseph and now his blood is required of them. But they did not know that Joseph understood because he was using an interpreter. And they said one to another, we are guilty concerning our brother, in that we saw the anguish of his soul, when he besought us, and we would not hear; therefore is this distress come upon us.

Joseph turned himself about from them, and wept; and returned to them again, and communed with them, and took from them Simeon, and bound him before their eyes. Then Joseph commanded to fill their sacks with corn, and to restore every man's money into his sack, and to give them provision for the way: and thus did he unto them. And they laded their asses with the corn, and departed thence. And as one of them opened his sack to give his ass provender in the inn, he noticed his money; for, behold, it was in his sack's mouth. And he said unto his brethren, My money is restored; and it is in my sack: and their heart failed them, and they were afraid, saying one to another, What is this that God hath done unto us? And they came unto Jacob their father unto the land of Canaan, and told him all that befell unto them.

And Jacob their father said unto them, Joseph is not, and Simeon is not, and ye will take Benjamin away: all these things are against me. And Reuben spake unto his father, saying, Slay my two sons, if I bring him not to thee: deliver him into my hand, and I will bring him to thee again. Jacob finally agreed to let Benjamin go with them when the corn was all gone and they needed to go and get more.

And when Joseph saw Benjamin with them, he said to the ruler of his house, bring these men home for they shall dine with me at noon. And the man did as Joseph asked; and the man brought the men into Joseph's house. And the men were afraid, because they were brought into Joseph's house; and they said, Because of the money that was returned in our sacks at the first time are we brought in; that he may seek occasion against us, and fall upon us, and take us for bondmen, and our asses.

Joseph commanded his servants to put his cup, the silver cup, in the sack's mouth of the youngest, and his corn money. And he did according to the word that Joseph had spoken. As soon as the morning was light, the men were sent away, they and their asses. And when they were gone out of the city, and not yet far off, Joseph said unto his steward, follow after the men; and when you overtake them, say unto them, why have ye rewarded evil for good? Now Joseph says to them that Benjamin must stay but Judah pleads on Benjamin's behalf.

Now when Jacob saw that there was corn in Egypt, Jacob said unto his sons, Why do ye look one upon another? [Gen 42:1 KJV]And he said, Behold, I have heard that there is corn in Egypt: get you down thither, and buy for us from thence; that we may live, and not die. [Gen 42:2 KJV]And Joseph's ten brethren went down to buy corn in Egypt. [Gen 42:3 KJV]But Benjamin, Joseph's brother, Jacob sent not with his brethren; for he said, Lest peradventure mischief befall him. [Gen 42:4 KJV]And the sons of Israel came to buy [corn] among those that came: for the famine was in the land of Canaan. [Gen 42:5 KJV]And Joseph [was] the governor over the land, [and] he [it was] that sold to all the people of the land: and Joseph's brethren came, and bowed down themselves before him [with] their faces to the earth. [Gen 42:6 KJV]And Joseph saw his brethren, and he knew them, but made himself strange unto them, and spake roughly unto them; and he said unto them, Whence come ye? And they said, From the land of Canaan to buy food. [Gen 42:7 KJV]And Joseph knew his brethren, but they knew not him. [Gen 42:8 KJV]And Joseph remembered the dreams which he dreamed of them, and said unto them, Ye [are] spies; to see the nakedness of the land ye are come. [Gen 42:9 KJV]And they said unto him, Nay, my lord, but to buy food are thy servants come. [Gen 42:10 KJV]We [are] all one man's sons; we [are] true [men], thy servants are no spies. [Gen 42:11 KJV] And he said unto them,

Nay, but to see the nakedness of the land ye are come. [Gen 42:12 KJV]And they said, Thy servants [are] twelve brethren, the sons of one man in the land of Canaan; and, behold, the youngest [is] this day with our father, and one [is] not. [Gen 42:13 KJV]And Joseph said unto them, That [is it] that I spake unto you, saying, Ye [are] spies: [Gen 42:14 KJV]Hereby ye shall be proved: By the life of Pharaoh ye shall not go forth hence, except your youngest brother come hither. [Gen 42:15 KJV]Send one of you, and let him fetch your brother, and ye shall be kept in prison, that your words may be proved, whether [there be any] truth in you: or else by the life of Pharaoh surely ye [are] spies. [Gen 42:16 KJV]And he put them all together into ward three days. [Gen 42:17 KJV]And Joseph said unto them the third day, This do, and live; [for] I fear God: [Gen 42:18 KJV]If ye [be] true [men], let one of your brethren be bound in the house of your prison: go ye, carry corn for the famine of your houses: [Gen 42:19 KJV]But bring your youngest brother unto me; so shall your words be verified, and ye shall not die. And they did so. [Gen 42:20 KJV]And they said one to another, We [are] verily guilty concerning our brother, in that we saw the anguish of his soul, when he besought us, and we would not hear; therefore is this distress come upon us. [Gen 42:21 KJV]And Reuben answered them, saying, Spake I not unto you, saying, Do not sin against the child; and ye would not hear? therefore, behold, also his blood is required. [Gen 42:22 KJV]And they knew not that Joseph understood [them]; for he spake unto them by an interpreter. [Gen 42:23 KJV]And he turned himself about from them, and wept; and returned to them again, and communed with them, and took from them Simeon, and bound him before their eyes. [Gen 42:24 KJV]Then Joseph commanded to fill their sacks with corn, and to restore every man's money into his sack, and to give them provision for the way: and thus did he unto them. [Gen 42:25 KJV]And they laded their asses with the corn, and departed thence. [Gen 42:26 KJV]And as one of them opened his sack to give his ass provender in the inn, he espied his money; for, behold, it [was] in his sack's mouth. [Gen 42:27 KJV]And he said unto his brethren, My money is restored; and, lo, [it is] even in my sack: and their heart failed [them], and they were afraid, saying one to another, What [is] this [that] God hath done unto us? [Gen 42:28 KJV]And they came unto Jacob their father unto the land of Canaan, and told him all that befell unto them; saying, [Gen 42:29 KJV]The man, [who is] the lord of the land, spake roughly to us, and took us for spies of the country. [Gen 42:30 KJV]And we said unto him, We [are] true [men]; we are no spies: [Gen 42:31 KJV]We [be] twelve brethren, sons of our father; one [is] not, and the youngest [is] this day with our father in the land of Canaan. [Gen 42:32 KJV]And the man, the lord of the country, said unto us, Hereby shall I know that ye [are] true [men]; leave one of your brethren [here] with me, and take [food for] the famine of your households, and be gone: [Gen 42:33 KJV]And bring your youngest brother unto me: then shall I know that ye [are] no spies, but [that] ye [are] true [men:

so] will I deliver you your brother, and ye shall traffick in the land. [Gen 42:34 KJV]And it came to pass as they emptied their sacks, that, behold, every man's bundle of money [was] in his sack: and when [both] they and their father saw the bundles of money, they were afraid. [Gen 42:35 KJV]And Jacob their father said unto them, Me have ye bereaved [of my children]: Joseph [is] not, and Simeon [is] not, and ye will take Benjamin [away]: all these things are against me. [Gen 42:36 KJV]And Reuben spake unto his father, saying, Slay my two sons, if I bring him not to thee: deliver him into my hand, and I will bring him to thee again. [Gen 42:37 KJV]And he said, My son shall not go down with you; for his brother is dead, and he is left alone: if mischief befall him by the way in the which ye go, then shall ye bring down my gray hairs with sorrow to the grave. [Gen 42:38 KJV]And the famine [was] sore in the land. [Gen 43:1 KJV]And it came to pass, when they had eaten up the corn which they had brought out of Egypt, their father said unto them, Go again, buy us a little food. [Gen 43:2 KJV]And Judah spake unto him, saying, The man did solemnly protest unto us, saying, Ye shall not see my face, except your brother [be] with you. [Gen 43:3 KJV]If thou wilt and our brother with us, we will go down and buy thee food: [Gen 43:4 KJV]But if thou wilt not send [him], we will not go down: for the man said unto us, Ye shall not see my face, except your brother [be] with you. [Gen 43:5 KJV]And Israel said, Wherefore dealt ye [so] ill with me, [as] to tell the man whether ye had yet a brother? [Gen 43:6 KJV]And they said, The man asked us straitly of our state, and of our kindred, saying, [Is] your father yet alive? have ye [another] brother? and we told him according to the tenor of these words: could we certainly know that he would say, Bring your brother down? [Gen 43:7 KJV]And Judah said unto Israel his father, Send the lad with me, and we will arise and go; that we may live, and not die, both we, and thou, [and] also our little ones. [Gen 43:8 KJV]I will be surety for him; of my hand shalt thou require him: if I bring him not unto thee, and set him before thee, then let me bear the blame for ever: [Gen 43:9 KJV]For except we had lingered, surely now we had returned this second time. [Gen 43:10 KJV]And their father Israel said unto them, If [it must be] so now, do this; take of the best fruits in the land in your vessels, and carry down the man a present, a little balm, and a little honey, spices, and myrrh, nuts, and almonds: [Gen 43:11 KJV]And take double money in your hand; and the money that was brought again in the mouth of your sacks, carry [it] again in your hand; peradventure it [was] an oversight: [Gen 43:12 KJV]Take also your brother, and arise, go again unto the man: [Gen 43:13 KJV]And God Almighty give you mercy before the man, that he may send away your other brother, and Benjamin. If I be bereaved [of my children], I am bereaved. [Gen 43:14 KJV]And the men took that present, and they took double money in their hand, and Benjamin; and rose up, and went down to Egypt, and stood before Joseph. [Gen 43:15 KJV]And when Joseph saw Benjamin with them, he said to the ruler of his house, Bring [these] men home, and slay, and make ready; for [these] men shall dine with me at noon. [Gen 43:16 KJV]And the man did as Joseph bade; and the man brought the men into Joseph's house. [Gen 43:17 KJV]And the men were afraid, because they were brought into Joseph's house; and they said, Because of the money that was returned in our sacks at the first time are we brought in; that he may seek occasion against us, and fall upon us, and take us for bondmen, and our asses. [Gen 43:18 KJV]And they came near to the steward of Joseph's house, and they communed with him at the door of the house, [Gen 43:19 KJV]And said, O sir, we came indeed down at the first time to buy food: [Gen 43:20 KJV]And it came to pass, when we came to the inn, that we opened our sacks, and, behold, [every] man's money [was] in the mouth of his sack, our money in full weight: and we have brought it again in our hand. [Gen 43:21 KJV] And other money have we brought down in our hands to buy food: we cannot tell who put our money in our sacks. [Gen 43:22 KJV]And he said, Peace [be] to you, fear not: your God, and the God of your father, hath given you treasure in your sacks: I had your money. And he brought Simeon out unto them. [Gen 43:23 KJV]And the man brought the men into Joseph's house, and gave [them] water, and they washed their feet; and he gave their asses provender. [Gen 43:24 KJV] And they made ready the present against Joseph came at noon: for they heard that they should eat bread there. [Gen 43:25 KJV]And when Joseph came home, they brought him the present which [was] in their hand into the house, and bowed themselves to him to the earth. [Gen 43:26 KJV]And he asked them of [their] welfare, and said, [Is] your father well, the old man of whom ye spake? [Is] he yet alive? [Gen 43:27 KJV]And they answered, Thy servant our father [is] in good health, he [is] yet alive. And they bowed down their heads, and made obeisance. [Gen 43:28 KJV]And he lifted up his eyes, and saw his brother Benjamin, his mother's son, and said, [Is] this your younger brother, of whom ye spake unto me? And he said, God be gracious unto thee, my son. [Gen 43:29 KJV]And Joseph made haste; for his bowels did yearn upon his brother: and he sought [where] to weep; and he entered into [his] chamber, and wept there. [Gen 43:30 KJV]And he washed his face, and went out, and refrained himself, and said, Set on bread. [Gen 43:31 KJV]And they set on for him by himself, and for them by themselves, and for the Egyptians, which did eat with him, by themselves: because the Egyptians might not eat bread with the Hebrews; for that [is] an abomination unto the Egyptians. [Gen 43:32 KJV]And they sat before him, the firstborn according to his birthright, and the youngest according to his youth: and the men marvelled one at another. [Gen 43:33 KJV]And he took [and sent] messes unto them from before him: but Benjamin's mess was five times so much as any of theirs. And they drank, and were merry with him. [Gen 43:34 KJV]And he commanded the steward of his house, saying, Fill the men's sacks [with] food, as much as they can carry, and put every man's money in his sack's mouth. [Gen 44:1 KJV]And put my cup, the silver cup, in the sack's mouth of the youngest, and his corn money. And he did according to the word that Joseph had spoken. [Gen 44:2 KJV]As soon as the morning was light, the men were sent away, they and their asses. [Gen 44:3 KJV][And] when they were gone out of the city, [and] not [yet] far off, Joseph said unto his steward, Up, follow after the men; and when thou dost overtake them, say unto them, Wherefore have ye rewarded evil for good? [Gen 44:4 KJV][Is] not this [it] in which my lord drinketh, and whereby indeed he divineth? ye have done evil in so doing. [Gen 44:5 KJV]And he overtook them, and he spake unto them these same words. [Gen 44:6 KJV]And they said unto him, Wherefore saith my lord these words? God forbid that thy servants should do according to this thing: [Gen 44:7 KJV]Behold, the money, which we found in our sacks' mouths, we brought again unto thee out of the land of Canaan: how then should we steal out of thy lord's house silver or gold? [Gen 44:8 KJV]With whomsoever of thy servants it be found, both let him die, and we also will be my lord's bondmen. [Gen 44:9 KJV]And he said, Now also [let] it [be] according unto your words: he with whom it is found shall be my servant; and ye shall be blameless. [Gen 44:10 KJV]Then they speedily took down every man his sack to the ground, and opened every man his sack. [Gen 44:11 KJV]And he searched, [and] began at the eldest, and left at the youngest: and the cup was found in Benjamin's sack. [Gen 44:12 KJV]Then they rent their clothes, and laded every man his ass, and returned to the city. [Gen 44:13 KJV]And Judah and his brethren came to Joseph's house; for he [was] yet there: and they fell before him on the ground. [Gen 44:14 KJV]And Joseph said unto them, What deed [is] this that ye have done? wot ye not that such a man as I can certainly divine? [Gen 44:15 KJV]And Judah said, What shall we say unto my lord? what shall we speak? or how shall we clear ourselves? God hath found out the iniquity of thy servants: behold, we [are] my lord's servants, both we, and [he] also with whom the cup is found. [Gen 44:16 KJV]And he said, God forbid that I should do so: [but] the man in whose hand the cup is found, he shall be my servant; and as for you, get you up in peace unto your father. [Gen 44:17 KJV]Then Judah came near unto him, and said, Oh my lord, let thy servant, I pray thee, speak a word in my lord's ears, and let not thine anger burn against thy servant: for thou [art] even as Pharaoh. [Gen 44:18 KJV]My lord asked his servants, saying, Have ye a father, or a brother? [Gen 44:19 KJV]And we said unto my lord, We have a father, an old man, and a child of his old age, a little one; and his brother is dead, and he alone is left of his mother, and his father loveth him. [Gen 44:20 KJV]And thou saidst unto thy servants, Bring him down unto me, that I may set mine eyes upon him. [Gen 44:21 KJV]And we said unto my lord, The lad cannot leave his father: for [if] he should leave his father, [his father] would die. [Gen 44:22 KJV]And thou saidst unto thy servants, Except your youngest brother come down with you, ye shall see my face no more. [Gen 44:23 KJV]And it came to pass when we came up unto thy servant my father, we told him the words of my lord. [Gen 44:24 KJV]And our *father said, Go again, [and] buy us a little food. [Gen 44:25 KJV]And we said, We cannot go down: if our youngest brother be with us, then will we go down: for we may not see the man's face, except our youngest brother [be] with us. [Gen 44:26 KJV]And thy servant my father said unto us, Ye know that my wife bare me two [sons]: [Gen 44:27 KJV]And the one went out from me, and I said, Surely he is torn in pieces; and I saw him not since: [Gen 44:28 KJV]And if ye take this also from me, and mischief befall him, ye shall bring down my gray hairs with sorrow to the grave. [Gen 44:29 KJV]Now therefore when I come to thy servant my father, and the lad [be] not with us; seeing that his life is bound up in the lad's life; [Gen 44:30 KJV]It shall come to pass, when he seeth that the lad [is] not [with us], that he will die: and thy servants shall bring down the gray hairs of thy servant our father with sorrow to the grave. [Gen 44:31 KJV]For thy servant became surety for the lad unto my father, saying, If I bring him not unto thee, then I shall bear the blame to my father for ever. [Gen 44:32 KJV]Now therefore, I pray thee, let thy servant abide instead of the lad a bondman to my lord; and let the lad go up with his brethren. [Gen 44:33 KJV]For how shall I go up to my father, and the lad [be] not with me? lest peradventure I see the evil that shall come on my father. [Gen 44:34 KJV]*

CHAPTER 45

JOSEPH MAKES HIMSELF KNOWN TO HIS BROTHERS

Joseph identifies himself to his brothers and weeps before them. He asked about his father and they told Joseph that he was alive and well.

Then Joseph said to them be not grieved, nor angry with yourselves, that ye sold me: for God did send me before you to preserve life. For these two years hath the famine been in the land: and yet there are five years, there shall neither be earing nor harvest. And God sent me before you to preserve you in the earth, and to save your lives by a great deliverance. So now it was not you that sent me here, but God: and he hath made me a father to Pharaoh, and lord of his entire house, and a ruler throughout all the land of Egypt. Hurry and go up to my father, and say unto him, God has made me lord of all Egypt: come down unto me, tarry not: And thou shalt dwell in the land of Goshen, and thou shalt be near unto me, thou, and thy children, and thy children's children, and thy flocks, and thy herds, and all that thou hast: And there will I nourish thee; for yet [there are] five years of famine; lest thou, and thy household, and all that thou hast, come to poverty. And, behold, your eyes see, and the eyes of my brother Benjamin, that it is my mouth that speaks unto you. And ye shall tell my father of all my glory in Egypt, and of all that ye have seen; and ye shall haste and bring down my father hither. And he fell upon Benjamin's neck, and wept; and Benjamin wept upon his neck. Moreover he kissed all his brothers, and wept upon them: and after that his brothers talked with him. And the fame thereof was heard in Pharaoh's house, saying, Joseph's brothers are here: and it pleased Pharaoh well, and his servants. And Pharaoh said unto Joseph, Say unto thy brothers, go to the land of Canaan; and get your father and your households, and come unto me: and I will give you the good of the land of Egypt, and ye shall eat the fat of the land. Now you are commanded take you wagons out of the land of Egypt for your little ones, and for your wives, and bring your father, and come. Also regard not your stuff; for the good of all the land of Egypt is yours. And the children of Israel did so: and Joseph gave them wagons, according to the commandment of Pharaoh, and gave them provision for the way.

And they went up out of Egypt, and came into the land of Canaan unto Jacob their father, And told him, saying, Joseph is yet alive, and he is governor over all the land of Egypt. And Jacob's heart fainted, for he believed them not. And they told him all the words of Joseph, which he had said unto them: and when he saw the wagons which Joseph had sent to carry him, the spirit of Jacob their father revived: And Israel said, It is enough; Joseph my son is yet alive: I will go and see him before I die.

Then Joseph could not refrain himself before all them that stood by him; and he cried, Cause every man to go out from me. And there stood no man with him, while Joseph made himself known unto his brethren. [Gen 45:1 KJV] And he wept aloud: and the Egyptians and the house of Pharaoh heard. [Gen 45:2 KJV]And Joseph said unto his brethren, I [am] Joseph; doth my father yet live? And his brethren could not answer him; for they were troubled at his presence. [Gen 45:3 KJV]And Joseph said unto his brethren, Come near to me, I pray you. And they came near. And he said, I [am] Joseph your brother, whom ye sold into Egypt. [Gen 45:4 KJV]Now therefore be not grieved, nor angry with yourselves, that ye sold me hither: for God did send me before you to preserve life. [Gen 45:5 KJV]For these two years [hath] the famine [been] in the land: and yet [there are] five years, in the which [there shall] neither [be] earing nor harvest. [Gen 45:6 KJV]And God sent me before you to preserve you a posterity in the earth, and to save your lives by a great deliverance. [Gen 45:7 KJV] So now [it was] not you [that] sent me hither, but God: and he hath made me a father to Pharaoh, and lord of all his house, and a ruler throughout all the land of Egypt. [Gen 45:8 KJV]Haste ye, and go up to my father, and say unto him, Thus saith thy son Joseph, God hath made me lord of all Egypt: come down unto me, tarry not: [Gen 45:9 KJV]And thou shalt dwell in the land of Goshen, and thou shalt be near unto me, thou, and thy children, and thy children's children, and thy flocks, and thy herds, and all that thou hast: [Gen 45:10 KJV]And there will I nourish thee; for yet [there are] five years of famine; lest thou, and thy household, and all that thou hast, come to poverty. [Gen 45:11 KJV]And, behold, your eyes see, and the eyes of my brother Benjamin, that [it is] my mouth that speaketh unto you. [Gen 45:12 KJV]And ye shall tell my father of all my glory in Egypt, and of all that ye have seen; and ye shall haste and bring down my father hither. [Gen 45:13 KJV]And he fell upon his brother Benjamin's neck, and wept; and Benjamin wept upon his neck. [Gen 45:14 KJV] Moreover he kissed all his brethren, and wept upon them: and after that his brethren talked with him. [Gen 45:15 KJV]And the fame thereof was heard in Pharaoh's house, saying, Joseph's brethren are come: and it pleased Pharaoh well, and his servants. [Gen 45:16 KJV]And Pharaoh said unto Joseph, Say unto thy brethren, This do ye; lade your beasts, and go, get you unto the land of Canaan; [Gen 45:17 KJV]And take your father and your households, and come unto me: and I will give you the good of the land of Egypt, and ye shall eat the fat of the land. [Gen 45:18 KJV]Now thou art commanded, this do ye; take you wagons out of the land of Egypt for your little ones, and for your wives, and bring your father, and come. [Gen 45:19 KJV]Also regard not your stuff; for the good of all the land of Egypt [is] yours. [Gen 45:20 KJV]And the children of Israel did so: and Joseph gave them wagons, according to the commandment of Pharaoh, and gave them provision for the way. [Gen 45:21 KJV]To all of them he gave each man changes of raiment; but to Benjamin he gave three hundred [pieces] of silver, and five changes of raiment. [Gen 45:22 KJV]And to his father he sent after this [manner]; ten asses laden with the good things of Egypt, and ten she asses laden with corn and bread and meat for his father by the way. [Gen 45:23 KJV]So he sent his brethren away, and they departed: and he said unto them, See that ye fall not out by the way. [Gen 45:24 KJV]And they went up out of Egypt, and came into the land of Canaan unto Jacob their father, [Gen 45:25 KJV]And told him, saying, Joseph [is] yet alive, and he [is] governor over all the land of Egypt. And Jacob's heart fainted, for he believed them not. [Gen 45:26 KJV]And they told him all the words of Joseph, which he had said unto them: and when he saw the wagons which Joseph had sent to carry him, the spirit of Jacob their father revived: [Gen 45:27 KJV]And Israel said, [It is] enough; Joseph my son [is] yet alive: I will go and see him before I die. [Gen 45:28 KJV]

CHAPTER 46

ISRAEL TAKES HIS FAMILY TO EGYPT

Israel packs up all he has and started out to go to Egypt and on the way he came to Beersheba and offered sacrifices unto The God of His father Isaac and God spoke to him in a vision of the night and said;

- I am God, the God of thy father: fear not to go down into Egypt; for I will there make of thee a great nation: I will go down with thee into Egypt; and I will also surely bring thee up again: and Joseph shall put his hand upon thine eyes.

And Jacob rose up from Beersheba: and the sons of Israel carried Jacob their father, and their little ones, and their wives, in the wagons which Pharaoh had sent to carry him. Jacob took all of his family with him and there were seventy of them that went to Egypt. The genealogy of the list of family that went to Egypt is listed in chapter 46. The number seventy is symbolic of the number prior to increase.

And Israel took his journey with all that he had, and came to Beersheba, and offered sacrifices unto the God of his father Isaac. [Gen 46:1 KJV]And God spake unto Israel in the visions of the night, and said, Jacob, Jacob. And he said, Here [am] I. [Gen 46:2 KJV]And he said, I [am] God, the God of thy father: fear not to go down into Egypt; for I will there make of thee a great nation: [Gen 46:3 KJV]I will go down with thee into Egypt; and I will also surely bring thee up [again]: and Joseph shall put his hand upon thine eyes. [Gen 46:4 KJV]And Jacob rose up from Beersheba: and the sons of Israel carried Jacob their father, and their little ones, and their wives, in the wagons which Pharaoh had sent to carry him. [Gen 46:5 KJV]And they took their cattle, and their goods, which they had gotten in the land of Canaan, and came into Egypt, Jacob, and all his seed with him: [Gen 46:6 KJV]His sons, and his sons' sons with him, his daughters, and his sons' daughters, and all his seed brought he with him into Egypt. [Gen 46:7 KJV]And these [are] the names of the children of Israel, which came into Egypt, Jacob and his sons: Reuben, Jacob's firstborn. [Gen 46:8 KJV] And the sons of Reuben; Hanoch, and Phallu, and Hezron, and Carmi. [Gen 46:9 KJV]And the sons of Simeon; Jemuel, and Jamin, and Ohad, and Jachin, and Zohar, and Shaul the son of a Canaanitish woman. [Gen 46:10 KJV] And the sons of Levi; Gershon,

Kohath, and Merari. [Gen 46:11 KJV] And the sons of Judah; Er, and Onan, and Shelah, and Pharez, and Zerah: but Er and Onan died in the land of Canaan. And the sons of Pharez were Hezron and Hamul. [Gen 46:12 KJV]And the sons of Issachar; Tola, and Phuvah, and Job, and Shimron. [Gen 46:13 KJV]And the sons of Zebulun; Sered, and Elon, and Jahleel. [Gen 46:14 KJV]These [be] the sons of Leah, which she bare unto Jacob in Padanaram, with his daughter Dinah: all the souls of his sons and his daughters [were] thirty and three. [Gen 46:15 KJV]And the sons of Gad; Ziphion, and Haggi, Shuni, and Ezbon, Eri, and Arodi, and Areli. [Gen 46:16 KJV]And the sons of Asher; Jimnah, and Ishuah, and Isui, and Beriah, and Serah their sister: and the sons of Beriah; Heber, and Malchiel. [Gen 46:17 KJV]These [are] the sons of Zilpah, whom Laban gave to Leah his daughter, and these she bare unto Jacob, [even] sixteen souls. [Gen 46:18 KJV] The sons of Rachel Jacob's wife; Joseph, and Benjamin. [Gen 46:19 KJV] And unto Joseph in the land of Egypt were born Manasseh and Ephraim, which Asenath the daughter of Potipherah priest of On bare unto him. [Gen 46:20 KJV]

And the sons of Benjamin [were] Belah, and Becher, and Ashbel, Gera, and Naaman, Ehi, and Rosh, Muppim, and Huppim, and Ard. [Gen 46:21 KJV] These [are] the sons of Rachel, which were born to Jacob: all the souls [were] fourteen. [Gen 46:22 KJV]And the sons of Dan; Hushim. [Gen 46:23 KJV] And the sons of Naphtali; Jahzeel, and Guni, and Jezer, and Shillem. [Gen 46:24 KJV]These [are] the sons of Bilhah, which Laban gave unto Rachel his daughter, and she bare these unto Jacob: all the souls [were] seven. [Gen 46:25 KJV]All the souls that came with Jacob into Egypt, which came out of his loins, besides Jacob's sons' wives, all the souls [were] threescore and six; [Gen 46:26 KJV]And the sons of Joseph, which were born him in Egypt, [were] two souls: all the souls of the house of Jacob, which came into Egypt, [were] threescore and ten. [Gen 46:27 KJV]

When Jacob arrived in Egypt he sent praise (Judah ahead of him) and they came to the land of Goshen. Joseph met his father there and wept upon his neck a long time. Joseph explained to his father what he would say to Pharaoh concerning his family and how they lived and what to say when Pharoah asks about their occupation and that he would request that they be permitted to live in the land of Goshen.

And he sent Judah before him unto Joseph, to direct his face unto Goshen; and they came into the land of Goshen. [Gen 46:28 KJVAnd Joseph made ready his chariot, and went up to meet Israel his father, to Goshen, and presented himself unto him; and he fell on his neck, and wept on his neck a good while. [Gen 46:29 KJV]And Israel said unto Joseph, Now let me die, since I have seen thy face, because thou [art] yet alive. [Gen 46:30 KJV]And Joseph said unto his brethren, and unto his father's house, I will go up, and shew Pharaoh, and say unto him, My brethren, and my father's house, which [were] in the land of Canaan, are come unto me; [Gen 46:31 KJV]And the men [are] shepherds, for their trade hath been to feed cattle; and they have brought their flocks, and their herds, and all that they have. [Gen 46:32 KJV]And it shall come to pass, when Pharaoh shall call you, and shall say, What [is] your occupation? [Gen 46:33 KJV]That ye shall say, Thy servants' trade hath been about cattle from our youth even until now, both we, [and] also our fathers: that ye may dwell in the land of Goshen; for every shepherd [is] an abomination unto the Egyptians. [Gen 46:34 KJV]

CHAPTER 47

JOSEPH REQUEST OF PHARAOH

Joseph did as he had shared with his father when it was time to address Pharaoh about this matter. Joseph took five of his brothers with him to meet Pharaoh; five is symbolic of the number of God's grace to man and responsibility of man. Pharaoh did ask them of their occupation and they responded as Jacob had told them to do. Joseph also brought his father to meet Pharaoh, Jacob blessed Pharaoh and Pharaoh asked Jacob his age, Jacob replied the days of the years of my pilgrimage are one hundred and thirty years: few and evil have the days of the years of my life been, and have not attained unto the days of the years of the life of my fathers in the days of their pilgrimage. Joseph placed his father and his brothers in Goshen, and gave them a possession in the land of Egypt, in the best of the land, in the land of Rameses, as Pharaoh had commanded. Joseph nourished his father, and his brethren, and all of his father's household, with bread, according to their families.

Then Joseph came and told Pharaoh, and said, My father and my brethren, and their flocks, and their herds, and all that they have, are come out of the land of Canaan; and, behold, they [are] in the land of Goshen. [Gen 47:1 KJV] And he took some of his brethren, [even] five men, and presented them unto Pharaoh. [Gen 47:2 KJV]And Pharaoh said unto his brethren, What [is] your occupation? And they said unto Pharaoh, Thy servants [are] shepherds, both we, [and] also our fathers. [Gen 47:3 KJV]They said moreover unto Pharaoh, For to sojourn in the land are we come; for thy servants have no pasture for their flocks; for the famine [is] sore in the land of Canaan: now therefore, we pray thee, let thy servants dwell in the land of Goshen. [Gen 47:4 KJV]And Pharaoh spake unto Joseph, saying, Thy father and thy brethren are come unto thee: [Gen 47:5 KJV]The land of Egypt [is] before thee; in the best of the land make thy father and brethren to dwell; in the land of Goshen let them dwell: and if thou knowest [any] men of activity among them, then make them rulers over my cattle. [Gen 47:6 KJV]And Joseph brought in Jacob his father, and set him before Pharaoh: and Jacob blessed Pharaoh. [Gen 47:7 KJV]And Pharaoh said unto Jacob, How old [art] thou? [Gen 47:8 KJV]And Jacob said unto Pharaoh, The days of the years of my pilgrimage [are] an hundred and thirty years: few and evil have the days of the years of my life been, and have not attained unto the days of the years of the life of my fathers in the days of their pilgrimage. [Gen 47:9 KJV]And Jacob blessed Pharaoh, and went out from before Pharaoh. [Gen 47:10 KJV]And Joseph placed his father and his brethren, and gave them a possession in the land of Egypt, in the best of the land, in the land of Rameses, as Pharaoh had commanded. [Gen 47:11 KJV]And Joseph nourished his father, and his brethren, and all his father's household, with bread, according to [their] families. [Gen 47:12 KJV]

The famine became more severe and there was no bread. Jacob gathered all of the money that was found in the land of Egypt and in the land of Canaan for the corn and brought all of the money to Pharaoh's house. Then the Egyptians came and asked for bread but they had not money and Joseph asked for their cattle, and when the cattle was gone Joseph gave them bread in exchange for horses and flocks, cattle of herds, for asses for that year.

The second year and this time they offered their land for they had nothing left but their bodies and their land. They offered their land to be servants of Pharaoh. And Joseph bought all the land of Egypt for Pharaoh; for the Egyptians sold every man his field, because the famine prevailed over them: so the land became Pharaoh's. And as for the people, he removed them to cities from one end of the borders of Egypt even to the other end thereof.

Then Joseph said unto the people, Behold, I have bought you this day and your land for Pharaoh: here is seed for you, and ye shall sow the land. And it shall come to pass in the increase, that you shall give a fifth part unto Pharaoh, and four parts shall be your own, for seed of the field, and for your food, and for them of your households, and for food for your little ones. And they said you have saved our lives: let us find grace in the sight of my lord, and we will be Pharaoh's servants. And Joseph made it a law over the land of Egypt unto this day, that Pharaoh should have the fifth part except the land of the priests only, which became not Pharaoh's.

Jacob lived in the land of Egypt seventeen years: so the whole age of Jacob was one hundred forty and seven years. And the time drew nigh that Israel must die: and he called his son Joseph, and said unto him, If now I have found grace in thy sight, put, I pray thee, thy hand under my thigh, and deal kindly and truly with me; bury me not, I pray thee, in Egypt: But I will lie with my fathers, and thou shalt carry me out of Egypt, and bury me in their burying place.

And [there was] no bread in all the land; for the famine [was] very sore, so that the land of Egypt and [all] the land of Canaan fainted by reason of the famine. [Gen 47:13 KJV]And Joseph gathered up all the money that was found in the land of Egypt, and in the land of Canaan, for the corn which they bought: and Joseph brought the money into Pharaoh's house. [Gen 47:14

KJV]And when money failed in the land of Egypt, and in the land of Canaan, all the Egyptians came unto Joseph, and said, Give us bread: for why should we die in thy presence? for the money faileth. [Gen 47:15 KJV]And Joseph said, Give your cattle; and I will give you for your cattle, if money fail. [Gen 47:16 KJV]And they brought their cattle unto Joseph: and Joseph gave them bread [in exchange] for horses, and for the flocks, and for the cattle of the herds, and for the asses: and he fed them with bread for all their cattle for that year. [Gen 47:17 KJV]When that year was ended, they came unto him the second year, and said unto him, We will not hide [it] from my lord, how that our money is spent; my lord also hath our herds of cattle; there is not ought left in the sight of my lord, but our bodies, and our lands: [Gen 47:18 KJV]Wherefore shall we die before thine eyes, both we and our land? buy us and our land for bread, and we and our land will be servants unto Pharaoh: and give [us] seed, that we may live, and not die, that the land be not desolate. [Gen 47:19 KJV]And Joseph bought all the land of Egypt for Pharaoh; for the Egyptians sold every man his field, because the famine prevailed over them: so the land became Pharaoh's. [Gen 47:20 KJV]And as for the people, he removed them to cities from [one] end of the borders of Egypt even to the [other] end thereof. [Gen 47:21 KJV] Only the land of the priests bought he not; for the priests had a portion [assigned them] of Pharaoh, and did eat their portion which Pharaoh gave them: wherefore they sold not their lands. [Gen 47:22 KJV]Then Joseph said unto the people, Behold, I have bought you this day and your land for Pharaoh: lo, [here is] seed for you, and ye shall sow the land. [Gen 47:23 KJV]And it shall come to pass in the increase, that ye shall give the fifth [part] unto Pharaoh, and four parts shall be your own, for seed of the field, and for your food, and for them of your households, and for food for your little ones. [Gen 47:24 KJV]And they said, Thou hast saved our lives: let us find grace in the sight of my lord, and we will be Pharaoh's servants. [Gen 47:25 KJV]And Joseph made it a law over the land of Egypt unto this day, [that] Pharaoh should have the fifth [part]; except the land of the priests only, [which] became not Pharaoh's. [Gen 47:26 KJV]And Israel dwelt in the land of Egypt, in the country of Goshen; and they had possessions therein, and grew, and multiplied exceedingly. [Gen 47:27 KJV]And Jacob lived in the land of Egypt seventeen years: so the whole age of Jacob was an hundred forty and seven years. [Gen 47:28 KJV]And the time drew nigh that Israel must die: and he called his son Joseph, and said unto him, If now I have found grace in thy sight, put, I pray thee, thy hand under my thigh, and deal kindly and truly with me; bury me not, I pray thee, in Egypt: [Gen 47:29 KJV] But I will lie with my fathers, and thou shalt carry me out of Egypt, and bury me in their burying place. And he said, I will do as thou hast said. [Gen 47:30 KJV] And he said, Swear unto me. And he sware unto him. And Israel bowed himself upon the bed's head. [Gen 47:31 KJV]

CHAPTER 48

THE BLESSING OF MANASSEH AND EPHRAIM

When Joseph heard that his father was sick he went to him and he took with him his two sons, Manasseh and Ephraim. Jacob began to tell Joseph what the LORD had promised him then Jacob said to him **And now thy two sons, Ephraim and Manasseh, which were born unto thee in the land of Egypt before I came unto thee into Egypt, are mine; as Reuben and Simeon, they shall be mine. They have a equal portion as if I had given birth to them. Any sons that you birth after these shall be yours. Now Joseph has the double portion that he had asked for when Ephraim was born because he named Ephraim the double.**

Jacob was old and not able to see well and he asked Joseph who are these and Joseph these are my sons and he brought his sons close to his father. Jacob said bring them here and I will bless them, but when Joseph saw that his father laid his right hand upon the head of Ephraim, it displeased him: and he held up his father's hand, to remove it from Ephraim's head unto Manasseh's head since Manasseh was the first born, then Joseph said unto his father, **Not so, my father: for this is the firstborn; put Your right hand upon his head. And his father refused, and said, I know it, my son, I know it: he also shall become a people, and he also shall be great: but truly his younger brother shall be greater than he, and his seed shall become a multitude of nations. And he blessed them that day, saying, In thee shall Israel bless, saying, God make thee as Ephraim and as Manasseh: and he set Ephraim before Manasseh. And Israel said unto Joseph, Behold, I die: but God shall be with you, and bring you again unto the land of your fathers. Here again we see the older brother serving the younger brother.**

And it came to pass after these things, that [one] told Joseph, Behold, thy father [is] sick: and he took with him his two sons, Manasseh and Ephraim. [Gen 48:1 KJV]And [one] told Jacob, and said, Behold, thy son Joseph cometh unto thee: and Israel strengthened himself, and sat upon the bed. [Gen 48:2 KJV]And Jacob said unto Joseph, God Almighty appeared unto me at Luz in the land of Canaan, and blessed me, [Gen 48:3 KJV]And said unto me, Behold, I will make thee fruitful, and multiply thee, and I will make of thee a multitude of people; and will give this land to thy seed after thee [for] an everlasting possession. [Gen 48:4 KJV]And now thy two sons, Ephraim and

Manasseh, which were born unto thee in the land of Egypt before I came unto thee into Egypt, [are] mine; as Reuben and Simeon, they shall be mine. [Gen 48:5 KJV]And thy issue, which thou begettest after them, shall be thine, [and] shall be called after the name of their brethren in their inheritance. [Gen 48:6 KJV]And as for me, when I came from Padan, Rachel died by me in the land of Canaan in the way, when yet [there was] but a little way to come unto Ephrath: and I buried her there in the way of Ephrath; the same [is] Bethlehem. [Gen 48:7 KJV]And Israel beheld Joseph's sons, and said, Who [are] these? [Gen 48:8 KJV]And Joseph said unto his father, They [are] my sons, whom God hath given me in this [place]. And he said, Bring them, I pray thee, unto me, and I will bless them. [Gen 48:9 KJV]Now the eyes of Israel were dim for age, [so that] he could not see. And he brought them near unto him; and he kissed them, and embraced them. [Gen 48:10 KJV]And Israel said unto Joseph, I had not thought to see thy face: and, lo, God hath shewed me also thy seed. [Gen 48:11 KJV]And Joseph brought them out from between his knees, and he bowed himself with his face to the earth. [Gen 48:12 KJV]And Joseph took them both, Ephraim in his right hand toward Israel's left hand, and Manasseh in his left hand toward Israel's right hand, and brought [them] near unto him. [Gen 48:13 KJV]And Israel stretched out his right hand, and laid [it] upon Ephraim's head, who [was] the younger, and his left hand upon Manasseh's head, guiding his hands wittingly; for Manasseh [was] the firstborn. [Gen 48:14 KJV]And he blessed Joseph, and said, God, before whom my fathers Abraham and Isaac did walk, the God which fed me all my life long unto this day, [Gen 48:15 KJV]The Angel which redeemed me from all evil, bless the lads; and let my name be named on them, and the name of my fathers Abraham and Isaac; and let them grow into a multitude in the midst of the earth. [Gen 48:16 KJV]And when Joseph saw that his father laid his right hand upon the head of Ephraim, it displeased him: and he held up his father's hand, to remove it from Ephraim's head unto Manasseh's head. [Gen 48:17 KJV]And Joseph said unto his father, Not so, my father: for this [is] the firstborn; put thy right hand upon his head. [Gen 48:18 KJV]And his father refused, and said, I know [it], my son, I know [it]: he also shall become a people, and he also shall be great: but truly his younger brother shall be greater than he, and his seed shall become a multitude of nations. [Gen 48:19 KJV]And he blessed them that day, saying, In thee shall Israel bless, saying, God make thee as Ephraim and as Manasseh: and he set Ephraim before Manasseh. [Gen 48:20 KJV]And Israel said unto Joseph, Behold, I die: but God shall be with you, and bring you again unto the land of your fathers. [Gen 48:21 KJV] Moreover I have given to thee one portion above thy brethren, which I took out of the hand of the Amorite with my sword and with my bow. [Gen 48:22 KJV]

CHAPTER 49

JACOB BLESSES ALL OF HIS SONS

And Jacob called unto his sons, and said; Gather yourselves together, that I may tell you that which shall befall you in the last days. They all came and Jacob gave a word to each one of them. This is where the rubber meets the road. Many of them probably did not expect what was said to them, but those that dishonored their father now understand what the end result of that foolish act.

And Jacob called unto his sons, and said, Gather yourselves together, that I may tell you [that] which shall befall you in the last days. [Gen 49:1 KJV] Gather yourselves together, and hear, ye sons of Jacob; and hearken unto Israel your father. [Gen 49:2 KJV]

- Reuben, thou [art] my firstborn, my might, and the beginning of my strength, the excellency of dignity, and the excellency of power: [Gen 49:3 KJV]Unstable as water, thou shalt not excel; because thou wentest up to thy father's bed; then defiledst thou [it]: he went up to my couch. [Gen 49:4 KJV]

- Simeon and Levi [are] brethren; instruments of cruelty [are in] their habitations. [Gen 49:5 KJV]O my soul, come not thou into their secret; unto their assembly, mine honour, be not thou united: for in their anger they slew a man, and in their selfwill they digged down a wall. [Gen 49:6 KJV] Cursed [be] their anger, for [it was] fierce; and their wrath, for it was cruel: I will divide them in Jacob, and scatter them in Israel. [Gen 49:7 KJV]

- Judah, thou [art he] whom thy brethren shall praise: thy hand [shall be] in the neck of thine enemies; thy father's children shall bow down before thee. [Gen 49:8 KJV]Judah [is] a lion's whelp: from the prey, my son, thou art gone up: he stooped down, he couched as a lion, and as an old lion; who shall rouse him up? [Gen 49:9 KJV]The sceptre shall not depart from Judah, nor a lawgiver from between his feet, until Shiloh come; and unto him [shall] the gathering of the people [be]. [Gen 49:10 KJV]Binding his foal unto the vine, and his ass's colt unto the choice vine; he washed his garments in wine, and his clothes in the blood of grapes: [Gen 49:11 KJV] His eyes [shall be] red with wine, and his teeth white with milk. [Gen 49:12 KJV]

- Zebulun shall dwell at the haven of the sea; and he [shall be] for an haven of ships; and his border [shall be] unto Zidon. [Gen 49:13 KJV]

- Issachar [is] a strong ass couching down between two burdens: [Gen 49:14 KJV]And he saw that rest [was] good, and the land that [it was] pleasant; and bowed his shoulder to bear, and became a servant unto tribute. [Gen 49:15 KJV]

- Dan shall judge his people, as one of the tribes of Israel. [Gen 49:16 KJV] Dan shall be a serpent by the way, an adder in the path, that biteth the horse heels, so that his rider shall fall backward. [Gen 49:17 KJV] I have waited for thy salvation, O LORD. [Gen 49:18 KJV]

- Gad, a troop shall overcome him: but he shall overcome at the last. [Gen 49:19 KJV]

- Out of Asher his bread [shall be] fat, and he shall yield royal dainties. [Gen 49:20 KJV]

- Naphtali [is] a hind let loose: he giveth goodly words. [Gen 49:21 KJV]

- Joseph [is] a fruitful bough, [even] a fruitful bough by a well; [whose] branches run over the wall: [Gen 49:22 KJV] The archers have sorely grieved him, and shot [at him], and hated him: [Gen 49:23 KJV] But his bow abode in strength, and the arms of his hands were made strong by the hands of the mighty [God] of Jacob; (from thence [is] the shepherd, the stone of Israel:) [Gen 49:24 KJV] [Even] by the God of thy father, who shall help thee; and by the Almighty, who shall bless thee with blessings of heaven above, blessings of the deep that lieth under, blessings of the breasts, and of the womb: [Gen 49:25 KJV] The blessings of thy father have prevailed above the blessings of my progenitors unto the utmost bound of the everlasting hills: they shall be on the head of Joseph, and on the crown of the head of him that was separate from his brethren. [Gen 49:26 KJV]

- Benjamin shall ravin [as] a wolf: in the morning he shall devour the prey, and at night he shall divide the spoil. [Gen 49:27 KJV]

All these [are] the twelve tribes of Israel: and this [is it] that their father spake unto them, and blessed them; every one according to his blessing he blessed them. [Gen 49:28 KJV]And he charged them, and said unto them, I am to be gathered unto my people: bury me with my fathers in the cave that [is] in the field of Ephron the Hittite, [Gen 49:29 KJV] In the cave that [is] in the field of

Machpelah, which [is] before Mamre, in the land of Canaan, which Abraham bought with the field of Ephron the Hittite for a possession of a buryingplace. [Gen 49:30 KJV]There they buried Abraham and Sarah his wife; there they buried Isaac and Rebekah his wife; and there I buried Leah. [Gen 49:31 KJV]The purchase of the field and of the cave that [is] therein [was] from the children of Heth. [Gen 49:32 KJV]And when Jacob had made an end of commanding his sons, he gathered up his feet into the bed, and yielded up the ghost, and was gathered unto his people. [Gen 49:33 KJV]

CHAPTER 50

THE DEATH AND BURIAL OF JACOB (ISRAEL)

And Joseph fell upon his father's face, and wept upon him, and kissed him. [Gen 50:1 KJV]And Joseph commanded his servants the physicians to embalm his father: and the physicians embalmed Israel. [Gen 50:2 KJV]And forty days were fulfilled for him; for so are fulfilled the days of those which are embalmed: and the Egyptians mourned for him threescore and ten days. [Gen 50:3 KJV] And when the days of his mourning were past, Joseph spake unto the house of Pharaoh, saying, If now I have found grace in your eyes, speak, I pray you, in the ears of Pharaoh, saying, [Gen 50:4 KJV]My father made me swear, saying, Lo, I die: in my grave which I have digged for me in the land of Canaan, there shalt thou bury me. Now therefore let me go up, I pray thee, and bury my father, and I will come again. [Gen 50:5 KJV]And Pharaoh said, Go up, and bury thy father, according as he made thee swear. [Gen 50:6 KJV]And Joseph went up to bury his father: and with him went up all the servants of Pharaoh, the elders of his house, and all the elders of the land of Egypt, [Gen 50:7 KJV]And all the house of Joseph, and his brethren, and his father's house: only their little ones, and their flocks, and their herds, they left in the land of Goshen. [Gen 50:8 KJV] And there went up with him both chariots and horsemen: and it was a very great company. [Gen 50:9 KJV]And they came to the threshingfloor of Atad, which [is] beyond Jordan, and there they mourned with a great and very sore lamentation: and he made a mourning for his father seven days. [Gen 50:10 KJV]And when the inhabitants of the land, the Canaanites, saw the mourning in the floor of Atad, they said, This [is] a grievous mourning to the Egyptians: wherefore the name of it was called Abelmizraim, which [is] beyond Jordan. [Gen 50:11 KJV]And his sons did unto him according as he commanded them: [Gen 50:12 KJV]For his sons carried him into the land of Canaan, and buried him in the cave of the field of Machpelah, which Abraham bought with the field for a possession of a buryingplace of Ephron the Hittite, before Mamre. [Gen 50:13 KJV]And Joseph returned into Egypt, he, and his brethren, and all that went up with him to bury his father, after he had buried his father. [Gen 50:14 KJV]And when Joseph's brethren saw that their father was dead, they said, Joseph will peradventure hate us, and will certainly requite us all the evil which we did unto him. [Gen 50:15 KJV]And they sent a messenger unto Joseph, saying, Thy father did command before he died, saying, [Gen 50:16 KJV] So shall ye say unto Joseph, Forgive, I pray thee now, the trespass of thy brethren, and their sin; for they did unto thee evil: and now, we pray thee, forgive the trespass of the servants of the God of thy father. And Joseph wept when they spake unto him. [Gen 50:17 KJV]And his brethren also went and fell down before his face; and they said, Behold, we [be] thy servants. [Gen 50:18 KJV]And Joseph said unto them, Fear not: for [am] I in the place of God? [Gen 50:19 KJV]But as for you, ye thought evil against me; [but] God meant it unto good, to bring to pass, as [it is] this day, to save much people alive. [Gen 50:20 KJV]Now therefore fear ye not: I will nourish you, and your little ones. And he comforted them, and spake kindly unto them. [Gen 50:21 KJV]And Joseph dwelt in Egypt, he, and his father's house: and Joseph lived an hundred and ten years. [Gen 50:22 KJV]And Joseph saw Ephraim's children of the third [generation]: the children also of Machir the son of Manasseh were brought up upon Joseph's knees. [Gen 50:23 KJV]And Joseph said unto his brethren, I die: and God will surely visit you, and bring you out of this land unto the land which he sware to Abraham, to Isaac, and to Jacob. [Gen 50:24 KJV]And Joseph took an oath of the children of Israel, saying, God will surely visit you, and ye shall carry up my bones from hence. [Gen 50:25 KJV]So Joseph died, [being] an hundred and ten years old: and they embalmed him, and he was put in a coffin in Egypt. [Gen 50:26 KJV]

Jacob died at the end of chapter 49 and now Joseph must keep his promise and burry his father where he had requested to be buried. And when Joseph returned from the funeral of his father and his brothers really pondered on their father being dead they thought that Joseph was only kind to them because of their father, and they sent word to Joseph asking his forgiveness and Joseph wept and told them to fear not, he said the evil you thought against me God meant it for good to bring to pass this day to save much people alive, he reassured them, and said fear not, I will nourish you and your little ones, he comforted them and spoke kindly to them.

He did ask them to take him with them when the LORD visited them and carried them out of Egypt. Joseph lived for one hundred and ten years.

This has been an interesting journey in the book of beginnings (Genesis). Understanding the beginning is the foundation for our understanding of the remainder of the books of the Old Testament. The history of the family of God is Adam's story and his story is our story.

DR. CYNTHIA V. WHITE

She graduated from Ballard Hudson High School in Macon, Georgia. She continued her education at Morris Brown College, Atlanta, Georgia where she received a Bachelor of Science Degree in Mathematics and Education. She has also received a Master of Arts in Biblical Studies, Master of Divinity and a Doctor of Ministry from Maple Springs Baptist Bible College and Seminary, Capitol Heights, Maryland.

Cynthia was employed by the Department of the Navy for 31 years. During her tenure there she was the head of the following departments: Computer Aided Design and Manufacturing, Industrial Improvement Technologies, Joint Electronic Drawings and Manufacturing of Industrial Data, Military Construction Projects, Service Craft Management and Manufacturing Technology Program Manager for Naval Shipyards. Cynthia is an accomplished conference speaker. She has spoken at the national productivity conferences, naval engineering conferences, research conferences, production conferences and general business conferences.

Cynthia is a strong supporter of community services. She participated in fund raisers for the March of Dimes, she supports children in need programs, she is a past Chairman of the Board of Directors of the Center for Community Development of Housing for the Mentally Ill and the Aged. She is also a past member of the Board of Directors of Bethel House, a community support center for people in need of help and assistance food, housing, education, jobs and other needs.

She is currently is a member of Heritage Church International, Waldorf, Maryland where Bishop Rodney S. Walker I. serves as senior pastor. Under Bishop Walker's leadership and covering Cynthia serves as the Secretary of Records of the church, Office Manager and past manager of Kingdom Christian Book. She serves on the staff of Heritage Church International as Chief Elder, the Overseer of the apostolic arm of the ministry and as an Associate Pastor. She has ministered as conference speaker for women, prophetic conferences, financial and business conferences and workshops. She has taught Bible Study at the Department of the Navy under the direction of the Chaplain for the Naval Sea System Command.

Accomplished Author

Understanding Spiritual Maturity

The Christian Torah – Kingdom Living the King's Way

The Importance of Seed

The Power of the Earth

Winning Battles with Love

What Your Father Never Told You About Business

The Sycamore Fig Tree – A Living Sacrifice

The Old Testament Survey – The Family of God – Genesis Manual

The Old Testament Survey – The Family of God – Genesis Workbook

Coming Soon:

The Old Testament Survey – The Family of God – Exodus Manual

The Old Testament Survey – The Family of God – Exodus Workbook

The Old Testament Survey – The Family of God – Leviticus Manual

The Old Testament Survey – The Family of God – Leviticus Workbook

The Old Testament Survey – The Family of God – Numbers Manual

The Old Testament Survey – The Family of God – Numbers Workbook

The Old Testament Survey – The Family of God – Deuteronomy Manual

The Old Testament Survey – The Family of God – Deuteronomy Workbook

The Old Testament Survey – The Family of God – Joshua – Song of Solomon

The Old Testament Survey – The Family of God – Isaiah – Malachi

Bible Trivia

The Bible at War

www.ingramcontent.com/pod-product-compliance
Lightning Source LLC
Chambersburg PA
CBHW080510110426
42742CB00017B/3064